Coming Out

A book for lesbians and gay men of all ages

Suzy Byrne and Junior Larkin

First published in 1994 by
Martello Books
An imprint of Mercier Press
16 Hume Street Dublin 2

Trade enquiries to Mercier Press
PO Box 5, 5 French Church Street, Cork

A Martello Original

© Suzy Byrne and Junior Larkin 1994

ISBN 1 86023 000 8

10 9 8 7 6 5 4 3 2 1

A CIP record for this title is available
from the British Library

Cover illustration and design by Brian
Finnegan
Set by Richard Parfrey in Lucida Bright
9/15 and Helvetica Black
Printed in Ireland by ColourBooks,
Baldoyle Industrial Estate, Dublin 13

To all those who have yet to come out and join our wonderful family

To David Norris – thanks!

To DBJ

To Adrian – RIP

Contents

Acknowledgements

Although I am used to spending a lot of time attached to a keyboard, the work put into this book has been quite a challenge for me. It would not have been possible without the following people so thanks to them all:

To my co-author and conscience, Junior for all his help, good humour and tea; to Mary Frances, the ever present straight friend who has put up with the late nights and the mess I leave for her to clean up in the morning, and thanks for putting up with the assumptions that she and I are lovers; to Nick Reilly for all his help in relation to the law and all the other bits of information he keeps in his brain; to the members of *Gay Community News* staff for their tolerance when Junior and I would be talking books; finally to the Gay and Lesbian Equality Network: Chris Robson, Kieran Rose, Eoin Collins and Feargus McGarvey, a group without the support of which I would not have been in a position to write this book in the first place.

Suzy Byrne

I know I have been a difficult person to live with while writing this book and for that I must apologise to my flatmates Paul and Ken and thank them for their help. Thanks to Richard Prenderville of *Gay Community News* for giving me so much time off work. Special thanks go to the members both past and present of Youth Group Dublin who have given me the motivation, and especially to Cathy, Darren, Paul and Rob who have carried the can in my absence. Thanks to my co-author and mentor Suzy who is still trying to get me interested in politics, to the National Lesbian and Gay Federation for helping me through some personal difficulties experienced because of writing this book, to Anthony McGrath for being Anthony, to my family for their tolerance and acceptance and last but not least to Brian Finnegan for his creative work on the cover design.

Junior Larkin

Introduction

If you are reading this book you are likely to be lesbian or gay or to have reason to believe that you might be. Perhaps this is a situation with which you are comfortable. More likely it is something that makes you nervous or uncomfortable. We all know that fear is a product of ignorance so this book is an attempt to dispel ignorance, to shed light on what it is like to be gay or lesbian in Ireland in the 1990s. It covers everything from the history of the Irish gay movements to the addresses of community and social groups that are available to help you if you need them.

As you will discover, coming out is not about standing in the middle of Dublin's O'Connell Sreet and screaming 'I'm gay'. It essentially involves your attitude to your own sexuality and knowing how to react to the situations that you may have to cope with.

The decriminalisation of homosexuality in Ireland has brought lesbian and gay issues out into the open. Some form of guidance is essential for people who think they might be lesbian or gay. In the absence of any formal education on the matter, this book attempts to provide the information you may need to make important decisions in your life. We have included the stories of some of the lives of Irish lesbians and gay men in this book; we thank them for their input. All names have been changed.

Irish society is changing fast. We document some of this change and indeed this, the first ever Irish guide to coming out, is part of the change. We were very conscious of the role of families, be they extended or nuclear, while we wrote this book. The International Year of the Family (1994) included diverse family units in its agenda. Unfortunately lesbian and gay families have yet to get a look in, as far as Irish society and the Irish celebrations of this year are concerned. By including chapters around lesbian and gay family units in this book we hope to have finally put this issue on the agenda.

We do not claim to know everything there is to know on the subject but we hope that what we have written will prove of benefit to you in your quest for knowledge and information. This book is aimed not just at young people who are coming out but at people of all ages and different stages of the coming-out process.

Suzy Byrne
Junior Larkin
Dublin, September 1994

1

Coming Out – Suzy's Story

It is probably an understatement to describe my childhood and teenage years as a sheltered existence. While my upbringing was not of the rigidly Catholic type, it wasn't far from it. I was alienated from other young people, both male and female, but totally unaware of the causes of this.

I was sheltered from the real world, although intelligent and willing to learn, aware of the world and issues in society. I knew I was not part of the heterosexual 'normality' expected of me and all those around me. When I was fourteen and yearning for knowledge about my body and those other forbidden facts of life, I knew I wasn't going to get married, have 2.4 children and be an adoring and submissive wife. I was afraid of what was going on in my mind and there was no one to tell.

I was a Catholic and loved religion, the ceremony and my participation in it. I read the lessons at Mass, and went on to be the youngest Minister of the Eucharist in my parish. I was probably the most pious student in my year at school. I was perceived by all around me, both parishioners and clergy, as the model young person – someone who would go on to great things no matter what I turned my hand to.

But I had great problems at school, particularly with my peers. I was different, too grown up for my age in some ways, although very innocent about sex and sexuality. I wanted to be closer to my female classmates. I had massive crushes on my teachers, particularly my English teacher who was a hockey-playing goddess and for whom I would have done anything. I didn't know then that lesbians existed. Being gay was to me a male 'disease'. I had been conditioned to believe that gay men were dirty and demented and that AIDS was the wrath of God. I did not question this but I began to question other moral issues. During my Leaving Cert year I fought with my parents about divorce, abortion and contraception because of the problems I had with the Catholic Church's teaching on these issues. Thus began a change in my thinking, as to me these were basic rights.

I finished school at sixteen and begged a male acquaintance to come to my debs, to keep up the show of normality. I still hadn't realised that I was a lesbian. I had no word or description for what I was. After a year of torment because of my lack of success in the dating game I left for England. A virginal Irish Catholic, I was shocked by the new culture. I was homesick, lonely and angry at my thoughts about being with other women. I began to read all around me while studying – books about assertiveness, the female orgasm, relationships, psychology. The new-found knowledge in what my mother called a *pagan* country began to take effect. I came across a book on teenage sexual experiences. These weren't ordinary teenagers, they were young lesbians and gay men. Suddenly a light went on in my dull brain, I rang the London Lesbian and Gay Switchboard and found out about a local lesbian and gay youth group. It was run by a youth worker and I arranged to see her before I went to the group. It was a great release, two and a half hours of tears and laughter, above all, a great feeling of not being 'strange' any longer.

I told no one at work about my new-found happiness. I went to youth group meetings and continued having counselling. I ventured out on to the scene and loved and hated it. I fell in love – well, it was really lust. Then I met Cathy, another Irish girl, in the laundrette. She wasn't anything special to look at, but then neither was I. We were at the same college but studying different things. First we became great friends; we were both loners and found we had a lot in common. It was weeks before we realised that we were more alike than we first thought. Our love deepened and we accepted each other for what we were. Bliss wasn't the word. Our relationship lasted three years, was strung over hundreds of miles and many visits and extravagant phone calls after I came home.

In Ireland, my secret life resumed. I began to work with young people. I still loved Cathy dearly but the distance between us became too much. I told none of my friends about my love. The Church still mattered to me but I knew that the members of the Church would not accept me for who I really was. I argued with members of the clergy about the Church's attitude to lesbians and gays. I had no contact with other lesbians and gays while I was in Dublin; I stayed in the closet for fear of persecution because of my work with young people. I wanted to rebel, to speak out to try to change people's attitudes to lesbians and gays, to add my voice to the growing call for changes in the law, but the attitude of the Church and its members stopped me.

A job interview and a vicious Vatican statement changed

all that. After many years of being alone, I had by then built up friendships with people who I regarded as safe to come out to. Indeed I have been lucky and the friends I have made, both straight and gay, have been very good to me. My work with young people continues, although my association with the Church came to an abrupt end. With so many years of repression behind me I wanted to make up for lost time and have committed the last two years of my life to being an activist.

Speaking out for basic human rights and being a visible lesbian in the media, writing about gay issues and meeting other lesbians and gay men from all over the world is now as much part of my life as my religion was when I was pretending to be straight. For me this is the way to express my pride in being a lesbian. I know that for many others there would not be the chance or even the desire to be as visible as I am. This was *my* way of coming out; there are many ways for different people. Busy making up for lost time, I am loud and proud after the years of silence and the torment of my youth, of not knowing what being a lesbian was.

I hope that this book will help you in your own way of coming out.

2

Coming Out– Junior's Story

I always knew I was gay. I had no problems with that but I knew that other people did have and would have. As far back as I can remember I was the object of verbal abuse and taunts by every Tom, Dick and Harry in the locality. It seemed at the time that there was a competition between them to see who could give me the most hassle or who could be *perceived* to give me the most hassle. The truth was that the jokes and name-calling mostly passed me by without leaving an impression. I was so used to hearing them that I didn't really notice them after a while.

When I was fifteen I fell in love with another boy from my school. Of course I knew I could never tell him or even hint to him how I felt. As it happened, though, we became good friends and it was he who eventually made the first move at forming a relationship with me. It was a relationship that, although immensely satisfying, was fraught with difficulties, especially having to hide behind a cloak of pretended heterosexuality with our school friends. Our partnership lasted for two years in all until eventually the pressure became too much and we split. He went on to date girls and is now in a longstanding relationship. At the time I was confused as to how he could date girls after being with another male for so long. His answer was that it was the person inside me that he was in love with and the fact that

I was a male didn't come into the equation. He has since stated that he would never be interested in a same-sex relationship again. We remain good friends to this day.

It was when that relationship initially broke up that I started to have my first major problems. I was in effect grieving for the relationship but as no other person had known of its existence there was no one I could talk to about it. I became sad, withdrawn, depressed, and nobody knew why. As time went on I got worse, yet still I couldn't bring myself to tell anyone why. I was afraid that I would also my other friends as well if they knew.

Things came to a head when I just couldn't handle anything any longer. The doctor put me on hefty doses of anti-depressants but these only succeeded in making me lethargic, not in lifting my spirits. I took an overdose and was admitted to hospital. After being pumped out I was retained overnight and made to see a psychiatrist before being released next morning. Regular visits to the psychiatrist/counsellor became a feature of my life but I still didn't divulge the real reason behind my depression. Homosexuality was never once mentioned. Eventually she moved away and I never kept any appointment with her replacement.

Months later I got back together with my boyfriend and things were great for a while. I gradually stabilised emotionally until my problems seemed but a distant memory. When the relationship came to an end for the second time, I knew that I couldn't possibly go through the grief on my own. On a night out with all my friends, I told them why I had been upset and instead of the rejection I expected I got nothing but support from them. They rallied round me and got me through the bad times. I know all this sounds like high drama but it must be remembered that we were teenagers and this was my first love – a hugely emotional time for anyone, whether gay or straight.

I swore all my friends to secrecy, forbidding them to tell a living soul. Of course some of them did tell people, mostly their parents, and suddenly I found myself having the benefit of adult advice when I needed it. Most of my friends at the time were girls and their parents accepted me completely; my male friends never told their parents about me. Being able to speak to adults really put things into perspective and it was a friend's mother who informed me about the gay community in Dublin. Up until that moment I didn't know that there was an organised community in Ireland. A male friend of mine offered to accompany me to a gay pub. It turned out that he was gay also; he just hadn't told anyone and thought it was the perfect excuse for him to make contact with other gay people without anyone suspecting. (It was his girlfriend's mother who told us where the pubs were!).

A few months later we heard about the gay and lesbian youth group in the city centre. We went along and loved it immediately and after a couple of visits I got involved in running it. This in turn introduced me to *Gay Community News* on which I became a voluntary worker. Still my family did not know anything about my being gay. I had no intention of telling them either and kept my activities outside of the house secret. In December 1992 I received an invitation, as Youth Group Leader, to meet the President of Ireland, Mrs Mary Robinson. I turned the invitation down as it would have meant telling my mother that I was gay. But when the chance to represent the Lesbian and Gay Community in the St Patrick's Day Parade in Dublin came up in March 1993, I decided that I wasn't going to miss it. So much had happened to me since I had joined the gay community that I felt strong enough to 'come out' at home. I knew I had plenty of support if I needed it. By now I was a paid staff member of *GCN*. My mother thought that I was doing a computer course (more lies) and didn't know anything of my involvement with the paper.

I sat her down with a cup of tea late one night and simply told her I was gay. The time was right. There was no way I could have stopped myself telling her; it just sort of burst out of me. I told her everything, about my involvement with the youth group and the paper and about my participation in the forthcoming parade. Time and time again I reinforced the fact that I had never been happier and that I was living a full and satisfying life. I had experience enough to know that this is what parents worry most about when they realise they have a gay child. All parents want their children to be happy but unfortunately they usually equate happiness with heterosexuality.

I'll just say that my mother wasn't very pleased at the time to find out that another of her children was gay. (I have a gay sister as well who was already out to the rest of the family although the subject was never mentioned and indeed I only found out when I told her that I was gay – which was two years after she had told the others.) A difficult couple of weeks followed where we were very polite to each other, neither of us knowing what to say and both of us trying to avoid the subject, until I realised that if I allowed this to continue I would in effect be putting myself back into the closet. Casual mentions of my work or my friends met with an icy response at first but as time went by she mellowed and even seemed interested at times. A few months later I started going out with a guy and although I didn't tell my mother this, she guessed the situation from seeing us together. Contrary to what I had expected, my mother was very nice to him, and although the relationship didn't last very long it gave me an indication of what I might expect for future relationships.

More recently and especially since I moved into my own place our relationship has improved dramatically. My mother expressed a lot of interest in my involvement in organising the International Lesbian and Gay Youth Conference in UCD and she even came out with me to a musical with a gay theme, *La Cage aux Folles,* and managed to enjoy it - *my mother!* Sitting in that theatre with my mother beside me watching two men kissing (albeit rather chastely) was a very special moment for me and, I think, for her. It helped show her that regardless of what some people say, same-sex relationships can work.

I know that sometimes my family would prefer it if I wasn't so open about my sexuality, I know that my openness can sometimes infringe their privacy and I fully appreciate the cooperation and support that I have received from them. My family is a very important part of my life and since I came out to them, we are able to share much more and play a bigger part in one anothers' lives. Once the secrecy went, so did the distance.

3

You Are What You Are

For each person, the process of coming out is different. There is no set way to go about it, no rules to follow and, more often than not, no access to details of other people's experiences. It is like a staircase with each stair being a step on the way, not to your final destination, but to the starting point of your new life. This new life will, it is hoped, mean an end to the need for secrecy, an end to your feelings of isolation and finally to a sense of belonging – of being part of a community.

We are not by any means saying that your life will miraculously become better overnight once you decide to come out. It is often a long and difficult process but it will be a definite improvement on your old life in the closet. On your way you will have to overcome a lot of prejudices and myths (some of which are explored and dispelled in this book). You may experience pain and rejection; alternatively you may find acceptance. These are things that you will not know until you embark on the journey. Unfortunately, because each person's experiences are different, we cannot give you specific advice or tell you exactly how to go about coming out. What we can do, however, is give you some general guidelines to help you through the process.

Yourself

Coming out as lesbian or gay is not just a simple statement of fact. It is a long, often painful, yet ultimately satisfying voyage, of discovery – both of yourself and of the world around you. It can happen at any stage of your life; it is not something that happens only to young people. Many lesbians and gays marry and have children before they pluck up the courage to reveal their true orientation. Some people never come out, living their entire lives under a veil of deception, in constant fear that their secret will be exposed.

Many people go through years of self-denial and feelings of worthlessness. This is because all their lives they are conditioned to believe that it is wrong to be lesbian or gay. Every television programme they watch, every newspaper they read and every advertisement they see is for, and about, the heterosexual majority. Most lesbians and gay men receive no acknowledgement of the existence of any other people like themselves as they grow up. When lesbians or gays are portrayed in the media it is usually as grossly inaccurate stereotypes. Thus the majority of lesbians and gays grow up feeling completely isolated

Quite often, gay people try to repress their natural feelings and desires in an attempt to blend in and be 'normal'. They don't want to be the way they are because they think it is somehow wrong. Thinking this way and repressing your feelings is what is wrong – not the feelings themselves. Your feelings are completely natural and perfectly normal. They are part of you and as such you must embrace them, not reject them.

It is unlikely that you will be able to live your life happily until you are able to accept your feelings. If you think that you are unable to do so on your own then you should get in touch with somebody who can help you. Counselling can be very helpful in this situation. Lesbian and gay switchboards are staffed by volunteers, all of whom have gone through experiences similar to your own. They are there to listen to you and provide advice where necessary, in a non-directive, non-judgemental way. Alternatively, if you can afford it and would prefer face-to-face counselling, your local switchboard will provide a list of counsellors in your area who may be able to help. There is no need to be afraid of counselling. A counsellor is just someone to talk to who understands your situation. The benefits that will accrue to you will far outweigh your initial embarrassment or fear.

It is often the sense of isolation that leads lesbians and gays into feeling there is something wrong with them. Often all that is needed to help you to accept yourself is some social contact with other people in your own situation. A visit to a group such as a Youth Group, Icebreakers or First Out meeting can be of immense benefit to you. Such an outing will reinforce your knowledge that you are not the only one, that other people are in the same situation as yourself.

Your family

You may think that you could never, ever, tell your family that you are lesbian or gay. Fear of rejection, of letting them down, of upsetting them all combine to stop you. People do not want to hurt their family and they fear that revealing that they are gay will do just that. Remember, though, that you are denying family members knowledge of a substantial part of your life. Not only are you denying them the opportunity to share in any happiness a relationship might bring you; you are also denying them the chance to help you with any pain or trouble you might experience.

Everybody has heard a horror story about someone who has come out and been totally rejected by their family but in fact this is comparatively rare. Parents usually react in confusion, not knowing what to do when they are suddenly confronted with evidence that they didn't after all fully know the child they have loved since its birth. Their initial reaction is not always the one to go by, as once they have had time to absorb what you have told them this attitude can change.

Don't forget: you have lived with the knowledge of your homosexuality for a long time. You have had the time to adjust to it, to get used to it. To your parents this is something new. It may be something that they have never even thought about or considered. Any information they might have on the subject is likely to be bits and pieces that they have casually learned from news reports or television over the years – and most probably negative reports at that. They will more than likely be worried for you; afraid that you are unhappy, alone, suffering. You must reassure them that you are none of these things.

Never tell your family until you are comfortable being gay. If you break down in tears as you tell them they are going to think that you are unhappy. This will automatically turn them against your being gay. Anything that upsets you upsets them. If you are unhappy or they think that you are unhappy then they will be unhappy also.

Before you tell them you must be prepared for every scenario. Ask a friend to be prepared to put you up for a while if necessary as your parents may take your news badly. Have the number of Parents Enquiry, a support group for parents of lesbian and gay children, ready to give your parents – they may not use it but it will be helpful as it will show them that they are not the only parents who have a lesbian or gay child. Remember that they will be experiencing much the same feelings that you had to go through at an earlier stage.

Take your time to explain things to them. Let them know about your life. They will probably have a lot of questions so be prepared to answer them calmly and as frankly as possible. If you are met with silence, don't try to force them to speak about it; give them the time they need to get used to it. The relief of getting it off your chest after having bottled it up for so long will make you want to talk about it. Try to contain yourself.

If they do take it badly and it becomes necessary for you to stay with a friend, leave them on their own for a few days before trying to make contact again. Let them know where you are so that they can get in touch with you if they wish to do so. Although this will be a highly emotional situation for you it is best if you try to remain calm when everyone else around you is letting their emotions take over.

David's story

I had been involved with Patrick for over a year when I decided that it was time to tell my parents that I was gay. The thought of it filled me with dread. It wasn't that they were overly religious or anything; it was just that they had always expected me to get married and give them grand-children. Patrick and I spoke about it and we decided it would be better if he wasn't around when I told them. I waited until I thought they were in a good mood before I said anything. At first they were in shock. They just sat there, not saying anything. Then they started to ask questions. How long had I been with Patrick? When did I know? What did I do? Where did I go?

I thought it was great. I mean, I was sitting there having a conversation, *a conversation*, with my *parents* about being *gay*, and they weren't shouting at me, they weren't calling me names, they weren't throwing me out of the house. As the weeks passed and they got used to the idea, they started treating Patrick and me the same way they treated my sister and her boyfriend. We were no different from them in my parents' eyes. They even invited him to Christmas dinner, which is strictly for family in our house. After all the deceit and the fear of telling them, I was actually really sorry that I hadn't done it sooner. I could have saved myself years of pain.

Charlotte's Story

There was really not a lot else I could do but tell my parents. I was afraid that other members of my family would find out by accident and tell them first. You see, I was twenty-four and the eldest in my family. We were all really close in age, the five of us. I had always been the awkward one. My twenty-two-year-old sister was getting married and my brothers were all going steady. Mam said that I did not go out enough to meet people. I always had something else to do, my studies or my running. I never brought anyone home to meet my family. Well, I couldn't, could I? My boy -friend didn't exist; I didn't even bother to make one up.

Sally and I had being seeing each other for three years, I had been involved in a lesbian swimming group and had also been going to women's venues for several years. Sally's family were OK about it. In fact they invited me to family gatherings. That was difficult for me to accept because I did not feel able to tell my family about our relationship. My family thought that Sally was a friend and that I was going out with her looking for a boyfriend.

Well, Dublin is a small place and someone was bound to find out sooner or later. The upstairs phone extension was the culprit. My brother picked it up when Sally rang one evening and he overheard our rather intimate conversation. (I had let my guard down as I didn't think that there was anyone else in the house.). He started dropping hints about lezzers and kd lang and I knew he knew. He said that he would tell Mam and Dad about me and they would sort me out.

A few weeks later after we had watched *Brookside*, I decided to tell my Mam. We were alone and I said that I had something to tell her. She asked if it was about Sally and me. I was stunned. Did she know what I thought she knew?

She said that she had realised many years before about me and that she gave up thinking that she would marry me off. She said that she had talked to some friends about me and that she was OK about it as long as I was happy and that I could talk to her at any time. I was so relieved. Why hadn't I done this a long time before?

We decided to tell my father. He was a bit angry at first, but my mother's acceptance of my life and my lover soon helped to bring him round. My brother shut up when he saw how tolerant the family was. I brought Sally as my partner to my sister's wedding. It was a bit awkward at first, but I soon relaxed. I'm happy now that this great weight has gone from my shoulders.

Your friends

You may decide to come out to your friends. It is by no means necessary for you to do so, especially if you are young, but friends are a great standby and by not telling them you are blocking off a potential source of support. You don't have to tell all your friends; you can choose one or perhaps a few close friends and you can ask them to keep it secret.

It is difficult to predict how people will react, even if they are long-standing friends of your own age. Perhaps some will not want to know you any longer, while sharing this know-ledge may help to bring you closer to others. Coming out to your friends will show you who your true friends are; the others may be only acquaintances. As with parents, however, you should allow your friends time to get used to the new situation; especially if it is something they never suspected, their initial reaction may be one of shock.

Francis's story

I was seventeen before I told anyone that I was gay. I remember the day as if it were yesterday. It was my best friends, John and George. I'd been with them for years and I just couldn't hold back any longer. We'd been talking about girls when I said it. I told them that I didn't fancy women, that I liked men. George went haywire, calling me all the dirty queers and faggots under the sun before storming off. John was brilliant about it though. He listened as I poured out everything that had been bothering me and he tried to give me advice. A couple of days later he came over to my house and told me that he'd rung Gay Switchboard and found out where there was a gay pub in town. He even came with me the first few times. These days he brings his girlfriend with him.

I never did get friendly with George again; I felt it wasn't worth the bother. If he couldn't accept that I was gay, that was his problem and he'd have to deal with it. I found out later that he was afraid that I fancied him!

John and I are still the best of friends, even better than before. I can talk to him about anything at all and he can do the same with me. I still haven't told my parents but I'm getting there. It won't be long now.

Your work

As with friends, it is not necessary to tell your work colleagues of your sexual orientation. You should tell them only if you feel, for whatever reason, that they should know

or if you would prefer them to know. You cannot be dismissed from your job simply because of your sexual orientation
so you need not worry about that. However, you may find
that workmates do not behave sensitively towards you if you
do come out and that you find yourself being the butt of
jokes in the cafeteria. This can be a difficult situation to
handle, especially if these jokes are made behind your back
but with your knowledge. There is only so much of this that
a person can take without responding to it and it is up to
you to decide what your response will be. See the chapter
on Rights and Wrongs for further information on harassment
in the workplace.

Liam's story

Working in a heavy machinery factory is quite a butch job,
I suppose. When I started I never even considered telling
anyone that I was gay. As far as I was concerned it was
something that they did not need not know; after all I don't
socialise with any of them outside work. As it happens, I
did tell one of the fellows on my shift. It just slipped out in
conversation, completely by accident. It didn't seem to faze
him at all; he didn't react either positively or negatively. I
suppose he just thought that it was none of his business.
Despite this I haven't bothered to tell anyone else in work
although all my family and friends know.

Lisa's story

I had been unemployed for a year after I left school before
I finally got a job. It wasn't much, just a junior secretarial
position, but it paid better than the dole. There was this
really nice guy working there and we soon became friends.
He was a great laugh so I didn't hesitate when he asked me

to go for a drink after work one night. In the bar he started coming on really strong. To say I was shocked would be putting it mildly – I really never expected it to happen, I thought he was just friendly. I made my excuses and left. Next day his behaviour towards me had changed. He kept on at me to go out with him. He couldn't handle the rejection. The following weeks were hell for me with him constantly harassing me. I felt there was nothing I could do about it. I was certainly not going to tell him I was gay because I couldn't be sure of his reaction.

I put in for a transfer to a different department and got it. On my first day there I quickly realised that there was a gay man among my fellow workers and that everybody knew about him and accepted him completely. I decided to come out and tell my new colleagues right from the start. It was no big deal to them and both my partner and I regularly go out with them as a group. Work is so much better now that I have nothing to hide.

There will probably come a time in your life when you feel that you can no longer keep your homosexuality a secret, no matter what the consequences. Only you will recognise when this happens and only you will know your own circumstances well enough to decide what to do. It is entirely your decision who to tell, when to tell and what to tell. Remember that telling people that you are gay doesn't mean that you have to tell them everything about your life. After all, it is unlikely that people would know everything about their straight friends or family members.

4

Step Back in Time

In the 1990s, almost every country in the Western world has a well established lesbian and gay community, but it wasn't always so. Indeed the idea of a person *being* lesbian or gay as a central part of her or his identity didn't even exist until the twentieth century. Of course, same-sex love did exist before the current century but society didn't focus on people's sexual identity as it does today.

The beginnings of lesbian and gay community identity

It was shortly after World War II that what was perhaps the world's first visible lesbian and gay community came into existence. During the war, millions of small-town American men and women were drafted into the armed forces or the workforce for the war effort. They were therefore obliged to live apart from their families and placed in single-sex environments. This gave lesbians and gays the chance to form same-sex relationships that they would never have had the chance to experience in their home towns. San Fransisco was at that time a major sea-port and the location of important war industries, staffed mainly by women. After the war many demobilised gay soldiers and marines, together with lesbians among the redundant female staff, decided to stay on there and build lives for themselves rather than return to their repressive small towns. California was, besides, the only state in the US where laws allowed lesbians and gays the right to meet in bars and other public places.

Small groups of gay people began to organise politically to campaign for equal rights. Among the first such organisations were the Mattachine Society and the Daughters of Bilitis, but these soon lost impetus and their members became disillusioned. The more radical strands of the gay and lesbian movement developed from the bars. One in particular, the Black Cat, featured a drag entertainer José Sarria, who, every Sunday, would finish his show by making political comments that fired the audience up. In 1961 José Sarria ran for the office of City Supervisor. He knew he had no chance of winning the election but that wasn't his objective anyway: 'I was trying to prove to my gay audience that I had the right, being as notorious and gay as I was, to run for public office, because people in those days didn't believe you had rights.' During his campaign, a group of gay men started to publish a bi-weekly newspaper, the *League for Civil Education News*. Although Sarria lost his election, his candidacy didn't go unnoticed, and by 1963 mainstream politicians had recognised the importance of the gay and lesbian vote and started to advertise in the gay newspaper.

However, all this political activity was very much confined to San Fransisco and lesbians and gays elsewhere continued their repressed and often isolated existences. In the lead-up to the Stonewall Rebellion in New York in 1969, black civil rights and women's rights groups were set up. Black militants led the way and showed other oppressed minorities how to turn their 'stigma' into a symbol of pride. This trigger-ed the setting up of new lesbian and gay groups. The rebellion of 1969, which saw gays, sick of police intimidation and homophobia, engage in violent clashes with police in the streets, changed the face of homo politics forever. Before the rebellion there were just fifty gay or lesbian groups in the whole of the USA; by 1973 there were eight hundred groups nationwide.

New strategies were developed. 'Coming out' as lesbian or gay became a political step and people who came out ex-perienced an almost immediate improvement in their lives when they cast aside the self-hatred and oppression engen-dered by a homophobic society. They also helped to build a mass movement; simply by being visible, they helped to draw thousands of other lesbians and gays to organise with them. By the mid-1970s, an infrastructure had been established, with publishing houses, community centres, health clinics and various shops and services catering for the lesbian and gay consumers.

Ireland

Not until 1974 did an organised lesbian and gay movement get off the ground in Ireland. The Irish Gay Rights Movement set up a Gay Centre in Parnell Square, Dublin, which provided a disco, social room, offices, telephone counselling line and a library. The IGRM later opened a disco in Cork but this survived only until 1981. In the late 1970s, a series of dis-agreements among the activists involved led to a bitter split in the movement. A rival organisation, The National Gay

Federation, was set up as a result. When the centre in Parnell Square closed down, the NGF set up its own base in Fownes Street and the Irish Gay Rights Movement reopened in opposition in Lotts Lane. The two centres went into competition. Obviously this situation was absurd, and to help solve the problem of the waste and duplication of resources, the first National Gay Conference was held in Cork in 1981. A huge success, the conference was attended by over 200 people and its decisions set the agenda for the 1980s.

The killing of a young gay man in Fairview Park in 1983 succeeded in putting the lesbian and gay campaign firmly back on track and in the public eye again. A gang of young men, although found guilty of manslaughter, were given suspended sentences and set free immediately, only to hold a triumphal march through the park. This conveyed the message to the public that it was somehow not a real crime to kill a gay person and enraged the lesbian and gay population of the country. A counter-march was organised under the banner 'Stop Violence Against Gays and Women' and received wide support from bodies such as women's groups, students, trade unions and progressive groups. At this time the constitutional amendment on abortion was being debated, so anti-amendment groups, sickened by the hypocrisy that was evident in the country, added their voices to the campaign. It was the biggest ever Irish march in favour of equal rights and gave new impetus to the gay movement in Ireland.

In the 1980s, Senator David Norris, a lecturer in Trinity College, Dublin, undertook a series of court battles with the Irish government in an effort to bring about the decriminalisation of homosexual activities. The case went as far as the Supreme Court and attracted massive publicity along the way. Having lost his fight to have such legislation declared unconstitutional in the Supreme Court by a majority decision, Senator Norris took the case to the European Court of Human Rights in Strasbourg. He won the case in 1988 and the Irish government was instructed to decriminalise homosexuality within a certain time-frame.

The fear of a right-wing backlash caused successive governments to request (and receive) extensions to this time-limit, and it was not until 1993 that homosexual acts ceased to be criminal. Significantly, it was the barrister who had taken the case for David Norris, Mrs Mary Robinson, by then President of Ireland, who indicated most publicly that Ireland was ready for change when she invited thirty-four representatives of the lesbian and gay community to her official residence, Áras an Uachtaráin, in December 1992. An intensive lobbying campaign, carried out in a responsible and determined way by the Gay and Lesbian Equality Network (GLEN), finally resulted in the Fianna Fáil-Labour coalition government passing reforming legislation on homosexual acts in 1993. (See the chapter on Rights and Wrongs for further details)

Ireland had started to come of age.

5

Some myths that need to be dispelled

There are, and always have been, a lot of myths and untruths about lesbians and gay men. Everybody has been exposed to these myths at some stage in their lives, often in the school yard – a place where misconceptions are absorbed as fact and carried on into later life. Below we take a look at some of the more widespread of these myths and balance them with the truth.

Gay men are effeminate

This is a very widely held belief. The most common media representation of gay men is that of the 'camp queen' and a result is that society thinks that all gay men behave in this manner. Even lesbians and gay men themselves sometimes hold this belief before they come out and meet other gay people. Obviously there are some gay men who do fit the stereotype – after all stereotypes have to have *some* basis in fact – but the vast majority of gay men look and act no differently from the average heterosexual male.

Lesbians are butch and masculine

As is the case with the gay male stereotype, the media's representation of lesbians has led to society thinking of them as being very manlike. Cropped hair and men's clothes is the image supposedly favoured by all gay women but once again this is untrue. Some lesbians do indeed dress this way but it is only one of many and diverse images that gay women adopt, just like their straight counterparts. This stereotype actually derived from the fact that many years ago, one half of a lesbian couple would sometimes act and dress like, and to all intents and purposes *be*, a man in public in order to fool people into thinking that the couple was, in fact, a heterosexual couple. Recently the new phenomenon of 'lipstick lesbians' has taken the media world by storm. It has now become almost chic to be both lesbian *and* glamorous. Who knows, maybe ten years from now lipstick lesbians will be the stereotype.

All gay men are transvestites

Another popular one, this. A transvestite (TV) is a person, usually a man, who has a need to dress as a member of the opposite sex and who, while so dressed, takes on a persona to match. According to the National Transvestite Line, the phoneline for TVs, the vast majority of TVs are heterosexual. The myth could have come from the tradition of 'drag' in the gay male community, where the art of female impersonation has been a form of entertainment for years. 'Drag queens' do not try to pass themselves off as real women,but rather tend to caricature ultra-glamorous showbiz stars. There is a saying: 'Not all gay men are drag queens, but all drag queens are gay men.'

Lesbians hate men and gay men hate women

Believing this is as misguided as believing that straight men hate other men and straight women hate other women. Just because lesbians and gay men love members of their own sex doesn't mean they hate members of the opposite sex. While it is true that some lesbians prefer to socialise in women-only spaces, it is not true that these women are man-haters.

Gay men are promiscuous

This one gets dragged out and used against the gay community time and time again. Gay men are no more promiscuous than straight men would be if straight women allowed them to be so. Another reason for this myth is that the gay community is smaller than the straight community and any sexual activity that takes place within it is therefore more noticeable to an outsider looking in.

Gay men are child abusers

All the research in this field show that child abuse is almost exclusively carried out by heterosexual males – usually on children who are closely related to them. Documented cases involving lesbians or gays are rare. Anyway people who are sexually attracted to children usually do not care what sex the child is; it is the age of the child that attracts them. These people are known as paedophiles and can be either heterosexual or homosexual.

Lesbians and gays lead a lonely existence

Lesbians and gays are no more likely to be lonely than their straight counterparts. People often think of gay people as being left on their own in old age because they haven't got a husband or wife. Many lesbians and gays are involved in long-term relationships and just because they haven't got a piece of legal paper to 'validate' this relationship doesn't mean that they don't consider themselves to be married. Those who are not in relationships usually have a large circle of friends to ensure they don't lead a 'lonely, solitary existence'.

Older lesbians and gays prey on younger ones

This statement comes up time and time again. Obviously if someone is young and attractive they are going to attract the attention of people of all age groups, not just of people in their own age group. This is true regardless of their sexuality. Let us not forget, though, that in order for an older gay man or woman to be involved with a younger person, the younger person has to be attracted to them in the first place. Just because someone is lesbian or gay doesn't mean that they are somehow condemned to have a sexual relationship with someone with whom they don't want to have one, which is what people are implying when they say that the older generation prey on the younger generation.

All gay men are disease carriers

This is a blatant lie spread in an effort to whip up prejudice against gay men. Gay men's bodies have nothing 'different' or 'special' about them that marks them out as 'better' disease carriers than straight men's. The gay world is considerably smaller than the straight world and any presence of sexually transmitted disease seems disproportionately significant. In fact, especially in recent years, gay men have tended to be more responsible than their straight counterparts when it comes to regular health screenings, so STDs are likely to show up in a larger proportion than in the straight population.

Lesbians and gays try to 'convert' straights

It is impossible to convert someone to being lesbian or gay, just as it is impossible to convert a lesbian or gay to being straight. If someone is not lesbian or gay by nature they cannot become that way just because someone else wishes them to be.

6

Lesbian or gay – born or made?

For years now there have been arguments as to whether people are born lesbian or gay or whether they are somehow made to turn gay. Many theories have been put forward by people supporting both sides of the argument and establishing the 'real' cause of homosexuality seems to be a burning issue. Strangely enough, though, it is usually heterosexuals who are caught up by the question, rather than lesbians or gay men.

Born lesbian or gay

A relatively modern way of thinking, this theory has grown in strength since its inception and refuses to be explained away. Much research has gone into proving that this is the true reason for the existence of lesbians and gay men, yet so far this research has not been conclusive. Recent advances in the field of genetic research have led some scientists to believe that they have indeed found a specific genetic code that makes men gay, a 'gay gene' as it has become known.

In 1993, Dr Dean Hamer, a National Cancer Institute researcher in San Fransisco, announced that he had identified a genetic pattern that predisposes towards male homosexuality. It seems then that we *are* born gay but this 'answer' led to even more questions:

- What if a test to determine if an unborn child is gay becomes available and pregnant women wish to abort. Should they be allowed to do so?
- Can governments continue to discriminate against members of society whose only crime was to be born with a certain genetic predisposition?
- What of the churches? Would they now change their attitude towards gay people?
- As the genetic code in question applied only to gay men, do we presume that lesbians are also born or is there still a question-mark over them?

These questions were given wide coverage in the mainstream media and a hot debate followed, with some surprising results. Some tabloid newspapers in Britain, traditionally among the most anti-gay in the world, led the call for new legislation protecting unborn children from abortion on the grounds of their apparent sexuality. They also called for new laws to make gays equal. How can we, they argued, justify discrimination against someone because of something over which they have no control? However, the tabloids soon returned to their homophobic views.

The Churches didn't really know how to take the news. One chief rabbi was quoted as saying that he would support abortion in this instance. He was widely condemned. The Catholic Church remained quiet at the time but the Pope went on to issue *Veritatis Splendor*, a document which sanctioned discrimination against lesbians and gays. (See chapter on religion.)

No new legislation was introduced in any country as a result of these findings and now Dr Hamer has begun similar research into lesbianism.

Lesbians and gays themselves weren't sure how to react to news of the discovery. Wasn't this what heterosexual people had always wanted – a 'cause' for homosexuality – the idea being that if a 'cause' was found then a 'cure' could be found also. Would this lead to the elimination of homosexuality in the human race? Hitler and his obsession with eugenics and his 'super race' came to mind. Up to half a million lesbians and gay men were executed in Nazi concentration camps simply for being gay and many others were experimented on in an attempt to 'cure' them.

However, the genetic pattern discovered by Dr Hamer has been patented and he himself has promised that he will not allow any test to be developed to determine if someone is gay. There is in any case no conclusive evidence that this genetic pattern on its own is what makes men gay. It apparently only gives them a *higher* chance of being gay. More research is needed to discover if environmental circumstances also play a part in making someone gay.

'Made' lesbian or gay

Parallel to the genetic theory is the constructionist theory. Basically there are two lines of thought in this theory. One is that men turn gay if they have a dominant mother and a weak father and that women turn gay if they have a dominant father and a weak mother. The other stream of thought is that we are somehow 'converted' by other gay people (even if we don't know any!).

The dominant parent theory is difficult to apply in many

cases we know but there are many influential people, mostly in the psychiatric field, who believe it to be true and who even claim to be able to isolate a single event in a person's childhood that made him or her turn out to be gay.

The other side of the constructivist theory is the corruption or conversion notion. This holds that we are 'made' gay not by our relationship with our parents, but by other gay people who deliberately set out to 'enlist' us into their ranks. This theory seems to overlook the fact that there is normally a sexual attraction present before sexual activity can take place. If someone was genuinely 'persuaded' to engage in same sexual activity against their natural orientation, surely they would not then consider themselves to be lesbian or gay. This theory also suggests that those who believe in it consider homosexuality to be something that is so attractive and good that one experience will turn a heterosexual person against their natural orientation. Yet in a contradictory way, it is usually the people who believe in this theory who are the first to condemn homosexuality as dirty and disgusting.

James's Story

When I was coming out I went to my parish priest for advice. I'd been an altar boy and choirboy for years so I knew him quite well and respected his opinion. It wasn't like confession; this was an informal setting over tea in his house. When I told him that I was gay, he started questioning me about who had made me this way. I was a virgin at the time. I had never had a sexual experience of any kind and as far as I was aware I had never known any other gay person either. I explained this to him but he wouldn't believe me. He was convinced that I'd been 'tampered with', and nothing could change his mind. He kept saying that homosexuality was wrong, abnormal and abhorrent and that nobody in their right mind would wish to be a homosexual. If that was the case why was he saying that I wasn't really gay but merely wanted to be. I couldn't understand his reasoning then and I still can't understand it now. As far as I am concerned I am gay, have always been gay and will always be gay.

While this argument rages on, millions of lesbians and gay men are quietly getting on with their lives, unconcerned by the question. It may well be that there is no one answer. While researching this book we came across many lesbians and gay men who believed they were born that way. We also came across many who thought that it was their upbringing that made them turn out gay. Others, mostly women, say that they turned to members of their own sex for affection after experiencing heterosexual rape or abuse.

Enough time and energy has been wasted in trying to discover a cause for homosexuality: time and energy that might well have been better spent in trying to find a cure for homophobia.

Rights and Wrongs – the Law

For decades, laws have discriminated against lesbians and gay men. They have either outlawed sexual practices or failed to protect us from unfair dismissals or other forms of discrimination in employment. Lesbian sex was never criminalised, although the reasoning behind this is widely believed to be the scepticism of Queen Victoria that love between women in a sexual way was possible. Nineteenth-century legislation criminalised all sexual acts between men, commonly referred to as sodomy and buggery. The legislation was enforced until the 1970s, with many being sentenced to ten years in prison. The legislation also caused suicides in prisons as those facing trial could not face the shame of being exposed.

For over twenty years Irish lesbians and gay men have campaigned for reform of legislation that caused misery to many lives. Gradually the changes that they fought for in cooperation with other non-gay organisations came about. These mean that our rights as equal citizens of this state will be maintained.

Sex

Homosexual acts between men were decriminalised (made legal) in Ireland in 1993. This followed a five-year delay in implementing the ruling of the European Court of Human Rights that instructed the Irish government to change the law banning homosexual sex. Senator David Norris had previously fought cases in the Irish High and Supreme Courts to try to establish that the ban on gay sex was unconstitutional and that he was not being treated as an equal citizen. The Irish courts ruled against him, and he and his lawyers including Mary Robinson SC (now President of Ireland), took the case to the European Court of Human Rights in Strasbourg and won.

After five years of government dithering, the Minister for Justice, Máire Geoghegan-Quinn, introduced the Sexual Offences Act 1993, which made homosexual sex between consenting adults over the age of seventeen legal. Unlike British legislation, Irish legislation contains no special privacy laws and there is an equal age of consent. This means that anything heterosexuals can't do, homosexuals shouldn't be doing either (i.e. sex in public).

Lesbian sex

Even though there has never been legislation governing sex between women, lesbians who have sexual contact with a minor (under sixteen) can be arrested and cases have been taken against women in the past. Under-sixteens are considered not of an age to give their consent, and while many lesbians discover their sexuality before they are sixteen and may become sexually active, they are liable to investigation by gardaí and social services if discovered. This is independent of the recent decriminalisation legislation.

Cruising

Cruising is meeting other men in outside areas in parks and public toilets, mainly for anonymous sex. It can be dangerous and may be illegal, depending on what you are caught doing. People who become involved in cruising are sometimes those who are not out or comfortable about their sexuality or who have no access to other gay venues. Often those who cruise do not practise safe sex.

Cruising is a part of gay culture which has its origins in the illegality of homosexuality. Even though this is no longer the case, cruising is likely to continue as those who cannot accept their sexuality or those who simply enjoy cruising take to the outdoors to meet other men for sex.

Trouble with the law

In recent years gardaí have been maintaining a high level of surveillance on cruising areas and have been questioning and sometimes detaining those seen loitering in cruising areas, even if they are not involved in any sexual acts.

- If gardaí stop you and request your name and address, ask them why they have done so.
- You may be asked to accompany them to a garda station. Again, you are entitled to ask them why they want to take you there. You do not have to accompany them to the station unless you are being arrested and if you go there voluntarily you do not have to stay there unless you have been arrested. If you are arrested you must be told for what reason.

- If you are arrested you are entitled to make a phone call and have a solicitor appointed.

- Ask for a pen and paper to keep a note of anything that you say or that is said or done to you while under arrest and before you see a solicitor. You should wait until you see a solicitor before saying anything or making a statement. Gay Switchboards will have the names of sympathetic solicitors who will represent gay clients. There will also be a list in the garda station of solicitors who operate under the free legal aid scheme.

- The gardaí are entitled to ask you questions but unless you have been arrested under the Offences Against the State Act or the Criminal Justice Act you are not obliged to answer them. Do not sign a statement unless you are advised to do so by your solicitor.

- While you are being held in custody you have the right to be treated as a human being, to receive food and drink, to have access to toilet facilities and to receive proper rest and sleep.

- If at any stage you feel that you have not been treated properly you should tell your solicitor and lodge a complaint with the Garda Complaints Board.

Discrimination in the workplace

Hundreds of lesbians and gay men have lost jobs purely because of their sexual orientation. In many cases other pretexts are used to discriminate against us as employers may not have wished to be known as anti-gay. Sometimes promotions and training are denied to us purely because we are gay. Other employees may harass, slag or even blackmail us in the workplace simply because they know or think they know about our sexuality.

Frank's story

In 1985 someone from work saw me going into a gay bar and told my boss about it. He called me into his office and asked me if I was a 'faggot'. I said yes. He then said that he didn't want my type working for him (I am a sales executive) as we couldn't be trusted and were too camp. As I dealt with the public, he said, I would lose business for his company. I had been working there for only six months and I wasn't a member of a trade union, so I just took my cards and left. I found another job and although only one of my workmates knows that I am gay, I am not afraid if the others find out as the law has been changed and I can't be sacked just for who I love. Anyway attitudes are beginning to change and I don't hear as many anti-gay jokes in the workplace as I used too.

Gradually, policies and legislation were introduced in Ireland to protect people from dismissal. This was a result of lobbying by activists from lesbian and gay groups in cooperation with the trade unions. Since 1988 civil servants have been protected from discrimination on the basis of sexual orientation or HIV status by a circular issued by the Department of Finance. In 1993 the Unfair Dismissals Act was amended to protect lesbians and gay men from being dismissed on the basis of their sexual orientation. This may not stop employers from stating other reasons for dismissal but with supportive legislation and the vast majority of Irish trade unions bringing in policies supporting our rights in the workplace we can challenge dismissals in this newly supportive atmosphere.

Issues surrounding promotions and training and harassment are due to be covered in an amended Employment Equality Act promised by the Programme for Partnership government. These issues may already have been dealt with under agreements negotiated by trade unions or equal opportunities policies.

Lesbians and gay men should not be dismissed on the basis of sexual orientation. It is crucial that we remember that legislation is now being introduced to protect us and there is now no reason just to let these abuses of our human rights go unchecked. The European Commission has recognised the fact that lesbians and gay men are more at risk of sexual harassment in the workplace also and they have recommended that member-states of the European Union enact legislation to protect us from harassment.

To protect your rights in the workplace
- Find out if your employer operates an equal opportunities policy which includes sexual orientation.
- If there are unions in your workplace find out what their policies are regarding lesbian and gay rights and join a union. In 1988, the Irish Congress of Trade Unions produced 'Guidelines on Lesbian and Gay Rights in the Workplace'. These guidelines state that 'lesbian and gay workers should be able to raise any issues (relating to recruitment and promotion and training, harassment and conditions of employment) with their union represent-

ative and expect them to be dealt with in a positive manner.'

What to do if you are sacked

- If you feel you have been unfairly dismissed and you have been employed for over a year you may be covered under the Unfair Dismissals Act 1993. Some categories of job are not covered under this legislation but they may be covered by their own equal employment policy.

- If you feel you have been dismissed because you are lesbian or gay or if you have been harassed at work, write down exactly what happened to you and any incidents of harassment or other unfair treatment you may have been subjected to, in or outside the workplace, from staff or management.

- If you wish to bring a claim for unfair dismissal ask your union representative for advice and assistance with lodging your claim. Alternatively you can pick up a form for this purpose from any FÁS office or labour exchange. The claim must be lodged within six months of dismissal and will be heard in private by a Rights Commissioner. If they find that you have been dismissed unfairly you may be reinstated or else awarded financial compensation depending on the merits of the case. Further information is available from the Rights Commissioner service.

Discrimination in other areas

Lesbians and gay men may face discrimination outside the workplace. Hotels may refuse to book a meeting space for gay groups. Landlords may try to evict tenants on the basis of their sexuality. Hospitals may deny partners visiting rights. A company may deny goods and services to lesbians and gay men. At the time of going to press, the government is preparing legislation that will prevent discrimination in non-employment areas. This legislation will protect not only lesbians and gay men but also women, ethnic minorities, people with disabilities and people with HIV or AIDS.

Partnership

At present there is no recognition of lesbian and gay relationships on a similar basis to heterosexual marriage. (Indeed, neither are non-marital heterosexual relationships recognised.) Many lesbian and gay couples want to have their partnership recognised as a symbol of their commitment to each other. They may also want to gain the same financial benefits as their heterosexual counterparts. Lesbian and gay couples face double taxation and are denied mortgage relief on the same basis as a married couple. Inheritance rights are not automatic in non-marital relationships.

An alternative opinion on the issue of partnership recognition is that lesbian and gay relationships should not be based on carbon copies of heterosexual ones, and that hundreds of partnerships have survived and will survive unrecognised by state or church.

In Norway, Denmark and Sweden couples can register their partnerships in a civil ceremony and gain financial benefits for a 'married' status. Before you think about rushing off to the Nordic regions with your loved one, it is best to know that only those who are resident in the country or who are citizens are entitled to this type of registration.

Until legislation is introduced that recognises lesbian and gay partnerships you may wish to perform your own 'commitment' ceremony with friends acting as witnesss and make your own vows to each other. Wedding services are available in Metropolitan Community Curches and lesbian and gay Christian groups in England. Further information may be got from London Lesbian and Gay Switchboard. In terms of achieving financial benefits you may wish to ask a financial adviser to investigate any options open to you. Ask your local Gay Switchboard or Lesbian Line for the name of a sympathetic adviser. Check to see if your employer grants benefits to non-married couples. Some companies operate such benefits and they may apply to all non-married couples regardless of sexual orientation.

Mortgage, life assurance + HIV tests

If you are applying for life assurance for a mortgage or other reason you may be asked if you consider yourself to be in a high-risk category for any illness. The insurance company or lender is really asking you if you are a gay man or otherwise at risk of contracting HIV. If you say yes to this question they will require you to undergo a HIV test. They will also ask you if you have ever had a HIV test before and even if you have had a test and the result is negative they will probably refuse to insure you or at best hike up your premium.

The reason for this discrimination against gay men is that insurers have overestimated the number of people who will be HIV-positive by the year 2000. Insurers want to cover themselves from paying out huge claims on the basis of this disease.

In operating this policy they do not recognise those who are responsible in practising safer sex or even those who are celibate. You may of course say no to any question about your sexual orientation or HIV status or whether you have ever been tested when applying for these services. But if you become HIV-positive after this, the insurer may cancel your policy if you answered no to the question. You may wish to consult an insurance broker to find out if there are any companies that do not discriminate against gay men. With the passage of the Maastricht Treaty many companies from Europe will be moving into the Irish market and some may be actively seeking out the pink pound. It is currently uncertain if legislation can be introduced to stop insurance companies from discriminating in this way. Lesbians are not discriminated against in this way as of the time of writing. Insurance companies have not yet investigated the risk factors surrounding lesbian health.

A report published by the a insurance federation in Britain has now recommended that questions about high-risk sexual practices should no longer be asked as the rates of HIV infection predicted in the 1980s have failed to materialise. The report recommends that the only question around HIV should be whether the individual is HIV-positive or not.

In July 1994 legislation was passed in Ireland containing a provision protecting lesbians and gay men from discrimination when applying for medical (health) insurance. This is the result of the opening of the European market under the Maastricht Treaty.

Wills

Even if you do not think you have any assets to pass on to other people it is essential that you make a will to document your wishes if you die. Many lesbians and gay men do not make wills and often their last wishes are not carried out as families take over and leave partners out in the cold. As the legal system does not recognise lesbian or gay relationships, if you do not make a will your estate automatically goes to your next of kin, in many cases your parents. Members of your family (even if you have disagreements with them and have broken off contact) have rights over you (your body) and your estate if you have not made a will.

Wills are vital if you are a parent, as you may want to name guardians for your children. You may have bought a house or other valuable asset with your partner and may wish to leave your half to him or her. You can write your own will; forms are available in stationery shops. It is advisable, however, if children or large amounts of property are involved or indeed if you want to be very clear about your wishes regarding your funeral, that you contact a solicitor. Fees for drawing up a will are not prohibitive and may be well worth the outlay in the long run.

Incitement to hatred legislation

This legislation was enacted in Ireland in 1989 and protects lesbians and gay men from those who incite hatred. It was introduced by the government because they needed to ratify the UN treaty on civil and political rights. It is believed that anyone found to be making a speech or printing material in the public domain that incites hatred can be prosecuted under this legislation. No case has ever been taken under this law although several gay groups have submitted homophobic printed material for the attention of the Director of Public Prosecutions. It is also an offence to incite hatred on the grounds of race, colour, ethic origin, nationality or membership of the travelling community.

Custody

Some lesbians and gay men may have married and have had children. Upon the separation of the partners the issue of custody of the children often arises. The heterosexual partner may often use the sexuality of the other partner as a threat if the gay partner contests the custody. Many gay parents have not contested custody of their children as they fear being 'outed' and also may want to protect their children from the distress of an ugly court battle. There is no legislation at present dealing with custody of children where the sexuality of a parent is involved. Because many of the judges involved in ruling on these cases are male and over fifty they tend to interpret the law in a discriminatory manner. Homosexuality has never been proved harmful to the welfare of children and judges tend to rely on their own personal opinions when ruling against gay parents having custody of their children. They are often prejudiced by the case put by the heterosexual partner. If you are a gay parent who may be involved in a custody battle, contact your local Lesbian and Gay Switchboard as soon as possible to get contacts for specialist advice.

Finally

Much of the information above may make you even more anxious about coming out. It is important to remember that thousands of lesbians and gay men in Ireland have come out before you and have faced worse oppression through being made criminal. If you are lesbian or gay and coming out or thinking about it in the 1990s, regard yourself as very lucky to be coming out in a changing Ireland. Remember if you have a problem talk to someone about it, be they in a lesbian or gay group or a professional organisation. You will not be the first or last person to have trouble with the law.

8 Religion

The Bible – the basis for religious views on homosexuality

When asked to justify its continued prejudice against lesbian and gay people, the Catholic Church often claims that homosexuality is, according to the Bible, an abomination. This, it is claimed, is sufficient reason to discriminate against gay people. However, Jesus never once mentioned homosexuality during his time on this earth, or if he did his words must have been regarded as of no importance as they were never recorded in the gospels, or elsewhere for that matter. There are phrases in the Bible that have been construed as references to same-sex acts, often on the basis of translations made many hundreds of years after the Scriptures were originally written.

Abomination

Any mention of the word abomination in the Bible is often misconstrued to be a reference to homosexuality. However, in its original Hebrew form of 'to'ebah' it is used only in connection with cases of worshipping false gods. Let us remember here that the only rules were given by God himself were the Ten Commandments, the first of which stated that his people were to put no other idol before God.

Sodom and Gomorrah

In this story God sent two angels in human form to earth to investigate reports of sin in the two cities of Sodom and Gomorrah. In the preceding chapter of the Bible we read that Abraham made a bargain with God that if ten righteous people could be found therein the cities would be spared (Genesis 18: 23-33). When the angels reached Sodom, Abraham's nephew Lot offered them his hospitality. At this time there was what was known as the Law of Hospitality, which was a sin to break. This hospitality extended by implication to the security and protection of guests.

In Genesis 19: 1-11 we read, 'But before they lay down, the men of the city, the men of Sodom, both young and old, all the people to the last man, surrounded the house; and they called to Lot, "Where are the men who came to you tonight? Bring them out to us, that we may know them."' This is taken to mean that the men wanted to know the angels sexually as the word '*yada*' was used in the original Hebrew. '*Yada*' means to know thoroughly and is used on a number of occasions throughout the Bible in a sexual context. Lot offered his two virgin daughters to the crowd rather than break the law of hospitality but they were refused. The intention of the men of Sodom was to rape the angels. The cities were duly destroyed by God and this episode has been read as a condemnation of homosexuality.

However if we read Judges 19 we find another rape, in the town of Gibeath. Again the people of the town wished to rape a visitor and again a female resident was offered as a substitute. This time, however, the substitute was accepted and raped until she died. This rape, a heterosexual one, led also to the destruction of that town (Judges 20: 38-44), so what we do in fact learn from both these stories is that the cities were destroyed, not for homosexual acts, but for rape and for the violation of the law of hospitality. No one has suggested that heterosexual acts be condemned because of Judges 19; yet some are eager to condemn homosexuality on the basis of Genesis 19.

Leviticus

In the book of Leviticus the people of Israel were given a number of laws by God, one of which was: 'Thou shalt not lie with mankind, as with womankind; it is an abomination.' (Leviticus 18:22). We already know that abomination is linked to the worship of false gods so how can it be explained in this instance? In order to do so we must look at the context in which these laws were given to the Israelites. They were given as the Israelites travelled through hostile lands, inhabited by worshippers of the fire god Molech. The laws forbade them to do numerous things which might make them appear to be like the followers of Molech (committing abomination). Included in this 'forbidden' list were such things as beard trimming, tattooing, wizardry, idolatry and menstrual intercourse (having sex with your wife during her period).

At this time people believed that men were created in God's image and that women were created in the image of man. Women were the possession of men and if a man treated another man in the way he would treat a woman, then that would be insulting to God and God's image, the man. Thus it was blasphemous to 'lie with a man as with a woman'.

However, these laws were also there to teach the Israelites that it was impossible to be perfect and that there was a need for a perfect sacrifice to make up for their imperfection. When Christ came and gave his life, the perfect sacrifice had been made. The laws had served their purpose and were cancelled. Paul in his Epistle to the Galatians makes it quite clear, 'Since the perfect sacrifice has freed us from the condemnation of the law, we are no longer under the law's demands.' (3: 23–25) 'We who are of the faith are not to associate any longer with the teachings of the law.' (4: 30–31). 'In fact, if we attempt to live up to the law, we as much as call Christ foolish in that he died for nothing.' (2:21).

Homosexual acts are no longer condemned under criminal law yet are still condemned under Church law. Does it not follow then that beard trimming, tattooing and even a married couple making love during the woman's period should all still be condemned by Church law.

The Bible, which is still seen as the rulebook for the Catholic Church, was written for a different kind of society over two thousand years ago. This society, if the Bible is to be believed, was one where men sometimes lived to be hundreds of years old, where people were stoned to death and where ritual sacrifice of animals was commonplace. Hardly much in common with society today, has it?

The Catholic Church and homosexuality

In Ireland, the predominant Church has always been the Roman Catholic Church. This is reflected in almost every aspect of our day-to-day lives. The Church's beliefs and doctrines are not only widely taught but are in some cases even enshrined in our law, which means that even non-Catholics have to live by the rules of the Catholic Church.

The Pope is the spiritual leader of the Church and as such is believed to be infallible. It is generally acknowledged that the present Pope (John Paul II) is a staunchly conservative man whose outspoken and often outdated views have alienated millions of his flock. During his reign, the Catholic Church in the West has suffered an enormous haemorrhage of believers and millions of others have become 'wedding and funeral Catholics', going to church only on such big occasions.

Contrary to what might be expected in such a situation, the Church, instead of re-examining its role in modern society and adapting itself for survival, is continuing its attempt to control people's lives. Recent statements from the Vatican have fluctuated in their terms of abusive and patronising language. In 1992 a statement released for use by bishops in the USA said that homosexuality was a 'moral disorder' and that lesbians and gay men should not be allowed to work with young people or be sports coaches or serve in the military.

The world's bestselling book for 1994, the (all new and improved) *Catechism of the Catholic Church* details the treatment that should be given to 'those with homosexual tendencies'. It seems that now we should be treated with 'compassion, respect and sensitivity'. It looks as if we will be waiting a long time to be recognised as equal members of the Church without receiving 'special treatment', which is another term for a patronising and discriminatory attitude.

Many of us are hindered in coming out to our parents because we are familiar with our parents' beliefs and what they have been told and have learnt about homosexuality. Once they have accepted us for who we really are, many parents begin to resent the Church's diatribes and challenge priests and other religious on their homophobia. Others reject their children because of their inability to reconcile their religion and its teachings with their children's sexuality.

As well as homosexuality, sex outside marriage, divorce, contraception and abortion have all been favourite topics of the Irish hierarchy. Many Irish people now believe that all subjects relating to sex should, by rights, be a private matter for individuals to handle as they see fit.

The church in the future

There is no doubt that both attendance levels and the number of priests are dwindling in the Catholic Church. Society has become far more liberal in the last thirty years and the Church's refusal to modernise its thinking has led to many people deciding that they can no longer give their support to what they see as an outdated institution. People no longer want to be led like sheep through their lives.

For those of you who may be struggling to reconcile being lesbian or gay with your Catholicism, you should take comfort in the knowledge that modern-day discrimination has no basis in scripture and that Christ himself gave us only two laws to live by: Love God. Love your neighbours as yourself. (Matthew 22: 37–40)

While we are not predicting the total acceptance of homosexuality, it is safe to say that more members of the Church are forming their own opinions on moral issues as they experience them or when they come to know someone involved in a situation of which the Church would disapprove. Catholics are beginning to think more critically about what the Pope and the hierarchy say.

Gay priests

It may seem surprising, but some gay men, especially those from rural areas, were traditionally drawn to the priesthood. Many saw it as a means of hiding their homosexuality – as priests aren't allowed to marry, nobody would ask any questions about their bachelor status. Others saw it is a way of somehow 'repenting the sin of homosexuality' and offering their lives up to the service of God.

Gay-friendly Churches

The Metropolitan Community Church is an almost exclusively lesbian and gay church. Formed in America, it now has branches throughout the world. This church does not discriminate against people on the grounds of sex or sexual orientation and its priests, or pastors as they're known, are both male and female. In America at the moment the Metropolitan Community Church seems to be attracting more and more heterosexual members who are disillusioned with mainstream religions.

Liberal priests are starting to speak out against the teachings of the Catholic Church. Perhaps the best known of these in Ireland is Father Pat Buckley, who although not supported financially by the Church, is running his own ministry. Father Buckley has given his blessing to a number of lesbian and gay partnerships and has stated on many occasions that he has no problem performing ceremonies for same-sex 'marriages'.

Although not strictly churches, Reach and the Julian Fellowship are Christian groups for gay men and lesbians respectively. These groups give Christian homosexuals the chance to meet and discuss their beliefs in a non-threatening situation. They are a great source of support for many who feel alienated by the Christian Churches.

Other Christian churches

Members of the Church of Ireland have been allowed for the most part to make up their own minds on moral issues. The Archbishop of Armagh, Dr Robin Eames, has supported campaigns for equality run by the Gay and Lesbian Equality Network. Very rarely do you hear Church of Ireland hierarchy or ministers speaking out against lesbian and gay sexuality. Other faiths to have supported equal rights for lesbians and gay men include the Society of Friends (Quakers) and the Progressive Jewish Community.

9 Education

For many years the Catholic Church has dominated Irish education. Although a great deal of good was achieved by these religious educators in many areas, it was rare for them to create an environment sympathetic to young lesbians and gays because Catholicism teaches that homosexuality is a sin.

For this reason, lesbians and gay pupils still, by and large, do not receive an education that encourages them to feel good about themselves. It is almost impossible for young lesbians or gay men to grow up with a positive self-image when they are told at school, during religion and sex-education classes, that there is something 'wrong' or 'unnatural' about them. They are already likely to feel isolated because of the lack of visible lesbians or gays among our peers, and this deepens the negative self-image they absorb from the educational system.

Heterosexual students, on the other hand, are not educated to understand their lesbian and gay fellow-students. We all know that people fear what they do not understand, and this leads to frequent bullying and victimisation of anyone who is suspected of being gay. The education of homosexual students is therefore frequently disrupted or they drop completely out of a system that does not cater for their needs.

Bullying

Many lesbian and gay students live a life of deceit and terror. They are in constant fear that their secret will be discovered and that people will despise or hate them. Secondary school students in particular feel the need to keep their lives secret from their peers. Boys and girls may talk endlessly in school or on social occasions about their latest love or who they 'got off with' at the weekend; through all this, the gay student remains miserably and self-consciously silent. Some lesbian and gay students feel the need to lie, and create a 'boyfriend' or 'girlfriend' for themselves to help disguise their true orientation. This may not really be a good option as it is difficult, without a great deal of preparation, to remember the stories you told, and you can wind up getting into deep water and being found out. People will suspect that you are lying, begin to wonder why and perhaps even guess that you are gay.

Bullying is a problem in all schools. For whatever reason, some students get a kick out of having power over others. Lesbian and gays are not the only victims of bullies but the suspicion that someone is lesbian or gay is sometimes enough to mark them as targets for the bully. This may be no more than a suspicion as it is impossible to say for definite that someone is gay or lesbian on the basis of appearance only, but if a student even slightly resembles the stereotype of the effeminate gay man or butch lesbian woman, they can very easily be labelled as gay by their peers, often without justification. These stereotypes, often so misleading, persist in society because they support the prejudices of homophobic people and they may still be trotted out for 'entertainment' value in comedy acts or on television.

If you are the victim of bullying at school, don't be afraid to do something about it just because you are gay. In other words don't think it is inevitable or even that you 'deserve' it in some way. Tell a teacher, a counsellor or the Principal. It is the school's responsibility to stop bullying, no matter what the apparent cause is, and most schools are very conscious of their responsibility in this area.

John's story

When I was in school a rumour went around that I had got turned on in the showers by looking at other blokes. It wasn't true but that didn't stop people believing it. It started with people whispering behind my back and moved on to graffiti appearing on the bog walls. Then one day after PE, we were in the showers when two of the other lads started calling me 'queer' and 'faggot' and saying that I needed to be taught a lesson for looking at them (which I wasn't doing). They grabbed me and dragged me, naked, into the toilet cubicle, and flushed my head down the toilet. It was horrible because whoever had used it just before hadn't flushed it. I felt sick for days afterwards.

Anyway I couldn't face PE after that and started bunking off school when PE was on the timetable. I liked bunking off; it meant that I didn't have to put up with constant slagging. Then I started bunking off on other days also. Eventually my schoolwork suffered. I knew that I had to do something about it so I went to the careers guidance teacher and told her. Within days the main offenders had been expelled. Just knowing that if it happened again I had some way of stopping it made me feel safer. Anyway the bullying more or less stopped when the ringleaders were thrown out. Either the other pupils were afraid to bully me because the consequences were too severe, or they didn't feel under any pressure to bully me any more.

Sex education

The possibility of being lesbian or gay has never been discussed as an official part of the sex education curriculum in Irish schools. Many students who have brought the subject up in class have been denied answers to their questions. The general assumption is that straight is the only way and of course many educators and those in school management (which still includes many religious) still believe that homosexuality is a choice or even a fashion trend. Some progressive schools and teachers have invited lesbians and gay men into classrooms to talk about their experiences and to answer students' questions on the topic. Several lesbian and gay groups offer an outreach service for this purpose and are only too willing to be invited. The right wing of course accuse these groups of 'recruiting' while failing to see that such pressurising is exactly what is going on in terms of the current heterosexual sex education provision.

This situation in schools is set to change with recommendations from the Department of Education that sexual orientation be included as a topic in the curriculum for those in the senior cycle of secondary schools. This may be too late for you but the future does seem brighter for lesbians and gay men in years to come.

Third level

Attending third level education is a means to coming out for many lesbians and gay men. Often moving away from home and being in an environment where you have the right to assert your independence provides this opportunity for those of us fortunate enough to achieve this level of education. But attending a college as a lesbian or gay man can also be a frightening experience if you feel that you are the only one on campus or if there is no lesbian or gay society for you to contact for support. Many colleges are small and located in small-town societies where gossip travels fast, ignorance is bliss and intolerance rules.

The majority of Irish universities now have lesbian and gay societies. Regional Technical Colleges have yet to see queers organising but plans are afoot to rectify this situation. The student movement in general has for many years included the debate about lesbian and gay issues as a priority in their work and campaigns. Many college societies have fought long hard battles with college authorities in order to be recognised and funded. These groups provide a safe space, social activities and information sessions for lesbian, gay and bisexual students.

The Union of Students in Ireland also provides support, funding and training for their officers in lesbian and gay issues. They organise a roadshow which travels to colleges and provides information for those areas which do not have a lesbian and gay society. A part-time officer is employed by USI to work on lesbian, gay and bisexual issues.

In college you can get in touch with the students union

welfare officer for help and information. If you are being harassed by students or staff, you can ask the officer for support and confidential advice and handling of the matter. No college or students union should stand for staff harassing students or vice versa and action will be taken by the students unions and usually also by the college authorities.

Lesbian and gay teachers

The teaching profession is a very threatening environment for many lesbians and gay men. It is fertile ground for such myths as that gay people are child abusers or recruiters. As long as the Catholic Church is involved in education and society at large still influenced by traditional family values, lesbian and gay teachers remain fearful of staff and pupils finding out about their sexuality. Harassment by students of teachers who they think might be gay is common. Many teachers dread going into work to face the taunts of bullying students, many of whom may be afraid of their own sexuality. The inevitable questions: 'Why aren't you married, Miss?' or 'Have you got a girlfriend, Sir?' or 'When was your first kiss?' will be difficult to deal with if you are unprepared. You will need support. Your teachers union can be of assistance in this matter, as well as helping you if you are the victim of harassment by staff. Gay Switchboards and Lesbian Lines are also familiar with these issues.

Recent Vatican statements have indicated the Catholic Church's opposition to lesbian and gay teachers, but teachers unions have reacted strongly against these statements, stating that no teacher should be discriminated against on the basis of sexual orientation. These unions ran some training seminars on lesbian and gay topics and gave full commitment on these equality issues.

There is nothing in the contract drawn up by the Department of Education that says a teacher has to be straight to teach. Schools with a Catholic ethos may contest this, saying that lesbians or gays would not be appropriate role models in education. Other 'deviants' including single parents have been sacked in the past for their incompatibility with Catholicism but it would be unfair to say that this is still the case nowadays. There have been no *public* cases of gay teachers being sacked. This of course is to be expected as it would be very difficult for such a person to come out without putting at risk their future employment prospects. The Department of Education probably would not stand for this type of discrimination, given the government's commitments to equality, and new employment legislation, due to introduced later this year, will further protect teachers. Those working in VECs are protected under agreements negotiated between local authorities and teachers unions.

Prospects in this area are improving and although the classroom may seem daunting for many there are changes on the way. If you enjoy your job at the moment, go on enjoying it. The situation in the classroom looks set to improve, no matter which side of the desk you are on.

10 Safer Sex

Life in the closet is often a solitary one, lacking in many things, not least of which may be an active sex life. Consequently, when people do some out and venture into the gay scene, they sometimes go through the 'feast after the famine' stage, that is a phase of having a lot of sex simply because it is now available after a long period of abstinence. The advent of HIV/AIDS hasn't meant that people have had to stop having sex; it has, however, made people switch their sexual behaviour to safer sexual practices.

What is HIV/AIDS?

HIV (Human Immunodeficiency Virus) is the name of the virus that can cause AIDS. Being HIV-positive means that a person has been in contact with the virus; it does *not* mean they have AIDS. AIDS stands for Acquired Immune Deficiency Syndrome. It is a more advanced stage of HIV infection. It is called a syndrome because it has a wide range of symptoms which may vary greatly from person to person.

How is it transmitted?

HIV is transmitted *only* in the following ways:

- Through the exchange of sexual fluids: semen (spunk), vaginal fluids (juices) and menstrual (period) blood
- Through the sharing of needles/syringes or other inject-

ing equipment
- From a woman to the foetus in her womb or during birth or through breastmilk
- Through transfusion of blood or blood products (Although since 1985 all blood donations and blood products have been rigorously tested for HIV.)

We cannot get the HIV virus from everyday contact with someday who is positive: sharing cups, glasses, cutlery, toilets. We cannot get it by touching someone who is positive.

We can reduce our chances of getting HIV by practising *only* safer sex.

What is safer sex?

Safer sex is any intimate activity that doesn't involve body fluids (blood, semen, vaginal juices, faeces) from one person entering the bloodstream of another. It by no means limits what people can do together sexually; in fact, it encourages people to be more adventurous in what they do and how they do it. There are far more safe practices than there are unsafe ones and if these are adhered to, there is no reason why you shouldn't have a long, healthy and fulfilling sex life.

What form does safer sex take?

Many people think of sex as the actual act of penetration or being penetrated but it is far more than that. Sex should be adventurous and fun; after all it is a recreational activity.
- Kiss your partner all over their body, everywhere, that is, except the anus and the vagina. We have erogenous zones everywhere on our bodies. Everyone has their

favourites. Take time to find your partner's and it will be worth it for both of you.

- Use your hands. Massage is an extremely erotic experience, particularly if you use oils. Once again, take your time and massage the whole body, using short feathery strokes and long, slightly heavier strokes alternately. Try not to be too predictable as to where your hands are going to land next. Half the fun for your partner will be the unexpected touch.

- Dress up. Who says you have to be naked to have sex? Dressing up (or, indeed, down) can lend an extra dimension to your sex life. Underwear, denim, leather and rubber are all favourites, as are special costumes like uniforms. Your imagination is the only limit so forget our inhibitions and get dressed for sex.

- Body rubbing, hugging and cuddling are all perfectly safe and enjoyable – and much more exciting than they sound! Try using lubricants or oils to make the experience more erotic, preferably something that won't stain your sheets.

- Videos, books and magazines can be used to add a bit of spice to your sex life. The more explicit ones are of course banned by the Irish censor but tamer versions are quite readily available in record shops, book shops and newsagents.

- Light spanking and bondage as part of roleplay can be used to add spice to a relationship. Both these activities are considered to be safe as long as the skin is not broken.

- Sex toys such as dildos are safe as long as they are not shared. Wash in hot soapy water between uses if they are to be shared or, alternatively, place a new condom on them.

- Open-mouth kissing is still considered safe. Although there are traces of the HIV virus to be found in saliva, it is in such minute quantities that it can't be passed on to your partner.
- Masturbation (wanking) together or wanking each other is completely safe as long as there are no cuts on the hand that vaginal juices or semen can get through.
- 'Fucking' or being 'fucked' between the legs is not risky. Once again, the use of a lubricant or oil can add to the pleasure experienced.
- Although not everyone's cup of tea, pissing on your partner or being pissed on is safe as long as no urine gets into your body. Never swallow someone else's urine; there are many health risks involved in this.

All the above are considered to be safe sex practices. There are certainly others. You should use your imagination but also use your commonsense if you are not sure whether something is safe or not.

Other activities are considered to be low-risk, that is, they do carry *some* risk as regards the transmission of HIV.

Low risk

- Oral sex – fellatio (sucking cock) and cunnilingus (sucking /licking the vagina) can be risky, as spunk, vaginal juices and menstrual (period) blood can carry the virus. If you or your partner has cuts or sores in the mouth, then the

HIV virus could get into the bloodstream. The use of a condom of dental dam (a small square sheet of latex) can reduce the risk. Flavoured condoms are available and will serve as dental dams if they are cut along the side.

- Fingering the anus or vagina is risky because of the possibility of blood, faeces or vaginal juices entering through cuts on the fingers. Well-filed nails reduce the risk, as does the use of lubricant. Surgical gloves can be worn to reduce the risk further.
- Anal/vaginal sex with a condom is low-risk provided that the condom does not burst. Always use a water-based lubricant such as KY Jelly, as oil-based lubricants like Vaseline destroy the rubber in condoms. It is essential that condoms be used properly so follow the instructions on the packet and *never re-use a condom.*

High risk

- Anal/vaginal sex without a condom is very risky. The virus can pass to either partner during unprotected intercourse.
- Rimming – kissing or licking the anus – is risky as blood or faeces can easily carry the HIV virus. This is also risky as regards the transmission of Hepatitis B.

As this list shows, there are far more safe or low-risk practices than there are risky ones. However, just knowing what is safe and what is not is not enough to protect you. You must *practise* safe sex all the time. Do not be afraid to talk to your partner about it, whether you are in a long-term or casual relationship.

When you first come out, you will probably be nervous,

especially when it comes to sex. It can be difficult to bring up the subject of safe sex, particularly if you are with a partner who is more experienced than you or if either of you have taken drink or drugs. It is very important, however, to let your partner know exactly what you will or will not do. Remember even if you have unsafe sex only once, that once could be enough. Just because someone looks healthy, this doesn't mean that they haven't been exposed to HIV. Remember other sexually transmitted diseases; safer sexual practices and discussing your sexual histories will protect you from these nasties as well.

The incidence of HIV/AIDS is relatively low in the Irish gay scene. This is because of the preventive and educational work done in the 1980s by those involved in the area. However, figures released in 1993 show an increase in the number of young gay men who are becoming HIV-positive. It would appear that this happened as a result of young men thinking that the AIDS crisis had passed and that it was now safe to have unprotected sex. It is *not* safe to have unprotected sex under any circumstances, no matter what your partner may tell you.

Safer sex doesn't mean that you can't have a full and satisfying sex life. It doesn't mean that you can have only one partner. It doesn't mean that you have to remain celibate. It does mean, however, being responsible for yourself, being careful, and last, but not least, being imaginative about sex.

Sexually transmitted diseases

STDs are any diseases acquired primarily through sexual contact. The organism that causes these diseases generally enters the body through the vagina, anus, urethra and mouth. You can catch an STD from sexual contact with someone already infected, especially during oral, anal or genital sex. Warm moist environments such as the mouth and vagina as well as the scrotal area provide prime areas for the transmission of such diseases.

How do I know if I have an infection?
Look out for any of the following symptoms:
- Soreness or itch around the vaginal opening/vulva area/ penis
- A discharge from the penis or vagina
- Pain when passing urine
- Pain in the lower part of you abdomen, especially if you are feverish
- Blisters or lumps around the genital area

Most infections are easy to cure or treat and have no long-term effects. This is not to say that if *untreated* these diseases cannot have long-term effect on our health. Some of the infections do not have any specific symptoms or may have symptoms which are similar to those of a cold or flu. Some of the diseases listed in this section are not technically STDs but are included because they can be transmitted to partners.

What do I do if I think I have an STD?
Don't wait until you are feeling ill before you do anything about it. For peace of mind, if you are sexually active with

more than one partner, you should go for a general STD check-up every three months. STD clinics are available in most urban areas. They are free and confidential and also provide safer sex information. At a clinic you will undergo a series of tests to diagnose any possible ailment and the treatment will be given accordingly. In Dublin there is a specific Gay Men's Health Project which has a clinic for gay men where counselling and safer sex advice are available. Vaccination against Hepatitis B is also available.

Crabs and scabies

Crabs are tiny parasitic lice that can live in pubic, facial and armpit hair. Scabies is caused by the scabies mite which burrows under the skin. Both scabies and crabs are very contagious and can be passed on through direct or indirect contact (sharing bedding, clothes, towels). It is important, therefore, that when you are treated for this your partners and housemates are also aware and treated if necessary. This is one of the infections that can be passed through a toilet seat as the adult crab can survive outside the body for over 24 hours. You will also need to treat your bedding and other linen with a specially prescribed lotion.

Trichomoniasis

Otherwise known as trich, this is a one-celled parasite that can be found in both men and women. Symptoms include a discharge that is yellowish-green or grey in colour and has a foul odour. If another infection is present along with trich, the discharge may be thicker and whiter. After diagnosis, treatment is usually in the form of antibiotics.

Non-specific vaginitis

This is the term given to a vaginal infection the exact nature of which cannot be determined by doctors after investigation. A common condition, it is also called Anaerobic Vaginosis because the bacteria that cause it survive without oxygen. It is characterised by a watery smelly vaginal discharge. Treatment is generally in the form of antibiotics.

Thrush

Thrush is normally present in the vagina or rectum and only becomes a problem when the chemical balance of the vagina is upset, causing itchiness and white lumpy discharge which looks somewhat like cottage cheese. While not a STD by origin, it can be transmitted between partners from the mouth, vagina or rectum. Thrush can be triggered by pregnancy, antibiotics, diabetes, soaps or bubble bath. Treatment is in the form of a suppository and mouthwash. Many women try to treat it naturally with some success, using a tampon dipped in natural yoghurt and inserted in the vagina to return the chemical balance to normal. (Remember to change the tampon often).

Gonorrhoea

'The clap' is caused by a bacterium which travels along the moist passageways of the genital and urinary organs and affects the cervix, urethra, throat and anus. Symptoms can be mild in women but become very severe if untreated. Itchiness around the genital area, an unusual discharge from the vagina or penis as well as discomfort when peeing and uncomfortable bowel movements are some of the symptoms involved. If left untreated this infection can lead to complication in the bladder and pelvic area.

Chlamydia

Has similar symptoms to gonorrhoea and is often transmitted in tandem with the latter. Studies have strongly indicated a link between chlamydia and Pelvic Inflammatory Disease, which can lead to infertility and other problems affecting the ovaries and fallopian tubes. In men the disease is often called Non Specific Urethritis and they will experience a burning feeling while peeing and a discharge from the penis.

Hepatitis

A virus which is on the increase in Ireland at the moment, sexually transmitted hepatitis comes in two forms: Hepatitis A and Hepatitis B. Hepatitis A is usually contracted through infected food or water. The virus is present in faeces, so anal/oral contact should be avoided. The symptoms resemble flu, and the infected person may look jaundiced. The infectious period ends before the appearance of these symptoms. If your partner has hepatitis you can get a injection to increase your resistance. A change in diet and avoiding alcohol will probably lead to a full recovery without any further effects and to immunity to Hepatitis A.

Hepatitis B is far more serious and may lead to permanent liver damage and sometimes death. Transmitted through the blood, the virus has been shown to be up to a hundred times more infectious than HIV. The symptoms can be very severe or just similar to a bad cold. Occasionally there may be no symptoms at all. The infected person may become lethargic, there may be swelling of the liver and pain in the joints. Again like in Hepatitis A the skin and eyes may yellow, there can also be changes in urine and bowel movements. The disease entails a long period of recuperation and often a stay in hospital is necessary. The infected person may still carry the disease and can infect others while appearing to be in full health.

Herpes

This is caused by two closely related types of virus. One type usually causes facial infection and infection of the throat or skin, the other usually infects the genital area or anus. It is possible to transmit one type of the herpes virus from the mouth to the genitals, or it can be transmitted on the fingers. Herpes is not curable, although the attacks may become less severe as time goes on.

Genital warts

It is believed that these are caused by the same type of virus that causes external warts. If untreated they can lead to cervical cancer in women. They are easy to treat either by painting a solution on or having laser treatment.

Syphilis

This is caused neither by bacteria nor a virus but by a separate organism called a spirochaete. This little devil can enter through the skin, either through the moist genital areas or even through fingers and lips. At the point of entry, the skin becomes swollen. After about three weeks a small blister appears and this can go unnoticed by many. The second stage of disease may also goes unnoticed or a rash may appear at this point. The organism may go into hiding and the disease may not be indicated on a blood test. During the third stage of the disease, which may never appear or could appear years after the spirochaete has entered your body, serious health complications including brain damage are possible. This disease is far less common than it used to be but you may have cause to worry about it if a partner has had a positive test or if you are unsure about sexual histories of partners. Treatment is generally in the form of antibiotics.

People who have a sexually transmitted disease are more susceptible to HIV, especially when they have sores or open cuts around their genitals. The body is working to fight the

STD and so has fewer defences against the virus.

Finally we do not mean to turn you off what may indeed turn you on. It is vital to realise that sex is about talking and negotiating with your partner as well as doing. So whatever you do, do it safely. Use a condom or a dental dam, take care of each other and take care of yourself.

11 Lesbian sexuality

Lesbians get a lot of stick, from men in particular, in relation to being lesbian. They say that we haven't met the right man and that all that we need is 'a good shag'. While we may all have an idea what heterosexual sex is from the basic sex education received in school and the bombardment of love scenes on film and television, the question of what lesbians do in bed can often be a fearful one for the lesbian who is just out or about to come out.

You may feel that you couldn't go to bed with another woman because you wouldn't know what to do. It is important to remember that sex is only part of being a lesbian and that often too much emphasis is placed on sex and what to do and where to put what and when. It is also important that you feel comfortable with your own body and your own image so that you have an idea of what feels good for you. There's no planting of the seed in lesbian sex and no need to worry about reproduction; and because we can learn about what turns us on through masturbation, there is much else that can become the focus for pleasure in a relationship. We need to think about who we are and recognise that sexuality is about more than what turns us on. It's about our attitudes, opinions and politics. While sex is about what we do, our sexuality is about who we are. We tend not to talk about either of these subjects among our friends and indeed even to our partners.

Because of religion and education and what our parents told us (and didn't tell us), we need to work at being comfortable with our bodies in order to explore our sexuality. Getting to know yourself will allow you to learn to enjoy and experiment with your body. Too often we see only the things we don't like about ourselves. The fact that our genitals are often part of what we don't like, that we are surrounded with taboos about our genitals and that menstruation is treated with disgust by society, makes it very difficult for women to like what we have been told not to touch and enjoy. It's a time to become independent of what society has trained us to feel.

Masturbation

Female masturbation is even less talked about than male masturbation. Women are not supposed to be turned on by themselves. Again we are reminded that we only masturbate because we can't get 'the real thing'. Masturbating is about pleasing ourselves, when and how we want to. It can happen when we are alone or as part of a sexual relationship. Often our first sexual arousal is that which we experience alone. We can use this time to find out what we like and perhaps tell our lovers about what works for us. If you have never masturbated before you may be affected by hang-ups deriving from your upbringing. Indeed you may be scared about what you might feel – or that you might not experience anything at all. Guilt about giving yourself sexual pleasure or fears about losing control may also be present in your mind. These common feelings will change in time.

At a time when you are alone and unlikely to be interr-
upted – maybe after a bath or shower – experiment with what
feels good. Maybe you could rub some oil into your skin,
choosing a scent such as lavender that relaxes you. Close
your eyes and touch all parts of your body; see which parts
excite you other than your cunt and your breasts; remember
what they feel like. Explore your cunt. Caress yourself using
different speeds and find out what feels good. Explore what
happens when you use different pressure. If you get wet,
taste your juices. As you become aroused you may feel your
muscles tighten. Your pelvic area may feel as if it were filling
up and your breathing may become faster. You may feel that
you are losing control and feel like letting go. If you have
an orgasm, think about what is feels like. (If you don't, don't
worry. It's an extra, not the only thing that is important.)
You can use a vibrator or sex toys if you like. Fantasies can
also play a part in masturbation. Remember that it is your
body and your feelings and you can experiment in any way
you like.

Making love to a woman

We return to that question which intrigues all, what lesbians
do in bed. Well, besides reading books and eating breakfast
that is...making love to a woman is not just a single
experience that can be put on these pages for you to read
and learn. Exploration is the key word. You need to find out
what you like doing and what your partner likes as well. Too
often we do not talk about what turns us on. Talking about
sex and experimenting with it are the most fun.

Women can have multiple orgasms so sex with another woman can last a long time. Foreplay is an essential part of sex and this can begin on the bus on the way home with the sensuousness of touch. Undressing each other, just holding and kissing can turn you on. Sharing a bath or a shower, towelling each other dry can help relaxation. There are no rules: we know what we like and we should not be afraid to tell our partner what does *not* make us feel good. There are numerous sexual practices popular with lesbians, many of which will not be detailed here, so this is definitely not an exhaustive guide. Touching, caressing, holding and kissing are the cornerstones and the boundaries are very wide.

Oral sex

Eating, licking, muff-diving, going down and sixty-nine-ing are among terms used by women to describe oral sex. It is an essential part of sex for many women and is based on mouth-to- genital contact. Many of us may feel scared about how we taste or afraid we might not like how another woman tastes. If you have not tasted your juices during mastur-bation, try it. You will find that making love with another woman will not taste so different. Remember that touching, caressing, kissing and holding are all important, and trying different speeds and pressures with your tongue will produce different responses. You can also use your fingers to excite her. Be careful to recognise any discomfort you may provoke if your partner's cunt becomes too sensitive. Be careful not to nick the delicate skin around her vagina with your teeth. There are lots of different kinds of enjoyment to be experienced but the above will help you to start out on a pleasurable journey for both of you.

Many women worry about not reaching orgasm or not bringing their partner to orgasm. Some are not upset about not reaching orgasm; they may be satisfied with pre-orgasmic feelings or indeed be in the process of accepting themselves. You may have had your first orgasm while masturbating. Remember what turned you on and show your partner how you bring yourself to orgasm. Remember what fantasies work and use them while lovemaking. You don't have to tell her that this is what you are doing but it may help you in your lovemaking. If you use a vibrator while masturbating, use it during lovemaking. Why not? Who says you can't?

Penetration

When the subject of penetration arises in talking about lesbian sex, many will say that all the woman wants is to be penetrated by a man. If you look at those all-important parts of your body, your hands, you will see that you have several different methods of penetration available. There are many ways of using your fingers during penetration. Many women enjoy the sensitivity and variety of positions available and of course there is a far better chance of fingers staying erect. However, women vary in the degree of pleasure they get from penetration.

Take care by removing any rings and making sure you have filed your nails and that there are no jagged edges. If you have any cuts on your fingers, cover them with plasters or wear a latex glove. You and your partner may want to use a lubricant such as KY Jelly to make penetration more comfortable. Do not use Vaseline or other oil-based lubricants inside the vagina. They cause irritation and may lead to infection; they can also break down latex gloves or dental dams that you use when you are practising safer sex and so increase the risks of STDs and HIV transmission.

Safe sex

You may feel uncomfortable going down on a woman who is menstruating (having her period) or if you are menstruating yourself. There is nothing wrong with oral sex during menstruation; it's just a bit messier. Women who are worried about HIV can use dental dams (square pieces of latex), cut open condoms or (non-microwave) Clingfilm as a barrier to prevent transmission. Transmission of HIV between women during oral sex is very rare, but low risk is not no risk, so it is essential to discuss the subject with your partner in order to protect yourselves if necessary.

Finally

- Feeling OK about yourself and your body is essential if you are to enjoy making love with someone else. Remember that this does not mean making yourself different or trying to look like someone else. You must accept and like yourself and your own difference.
- There are no rules for making love. No patterns, timetable or routine need apply to your lovemaking.
- There is a growing number of books on the subject that

you will find or can order from the lesbian and gay sections of the bookshops listed in the back of this book. They will not give you the definitive answers to your questions but they can give you more information than space permits here.

12 Gay Relationships

There is a popular misconception that lesbians and gay men do not have any relationships of note. Many believe that instead they engage in a neverending series of one-night stands with anonymous partners in loveless union. Balderdash!

Many lesbians and gay men can and do have loving, caring, long-lasting same-sex relationships that are fulfilling in every sense of the word. Not all these relationships follow the style of a typical heterosexual relationship but this does not mean that they are any less important or meaningful. There is a number of popular types of relationship forms within the lesbian and gay community, some of which we talk about in more detail here.

Monogamous relationships

These are perhaps the closest to the traditional form of relationship within society as a whole. In a monogamous relationship both partners agree to remain faithful to each other and forsake all others, the *mono* in monogamous meaning one. This is the type of relationship that we are most used to; the traditional heterosexual marriage is based on this model. It is important that both partners agree beforehand, as partnerships are likely to break up if only one partner is monogamous.

Non-monogamous relationships

These occur when partnerships are not exclusive. There are different ways to do this. For example, you can have two partners between whom you divide your time on an equal basis or you can have one 'important' partner and affairs on the side, similar to the 'open marriages' favoured by some heterosexual couples.

Regular sex partners

The person with whom you have this kind of relationsip is popularly known as a 'fuck buddy'. This type of partnership is when two people enjoy regular sexual intercourse without the limitations of a fixed relationship. It has become increasingly popular.

Roles in relationships

Many people believe that within same-sex couples, one partner takes on the male role and the other takes on the female role. Although there are, no doubt, some relationships that operate in this manner, by far the majority now operate on an equal, shared basis with neither partner taking on a specific role. Household chores are shared, as is the role of 'breadwinner'. In lesbian relationships especially, more and more women are rejecting the traditional roles and neither is assuming power over the other – as often happens with male-female couples.

Making relationships work

Once again specific advice cannot be given here as each couple will have problems and difficulties unique to them, but here are a few simple guidelines which seem to help.

- Lay down specific ground rules. If the relationship is to be monogamous then this must be stated from the beginning so as to avoid confusion later on. Don't expect to be able to change your partner; for example, if he/she is a smoker or heavy drinker don't think you can make them change their habits. They have to want to do this themselves.

- Try to keep ex-lovers out of your conversations. Mentioning them not only leads to jealousy (your partner wondering if perhaps you still have strong feelings for them) but it might also make your partner wonder what you would say about him/her in the event of a break up. By all means let your partner know about your history if they want to hear about it but try to avoid going into the specifics of your old sex life.

- Talk to each other. If something is bothering you then don't bottle it up; discuss it with your partner. This doesn't mean having a full-blown screaming match. If a row does develop be careful not to say anything in the heat of the moment that you may regret saying later. If you feel that you need some space on your own then say so. Don't just storm off without a word; let your partner know that you are going for a stroll or whatever.

- Trust each other. If you are honest with each other then you should have no difficulty in trusting each other.

- Don't neglect your family or friends. It is very important that a couple should retain their separate friends so that they are not together all the time. Nothing kills a relationship quicker than living in each other's pockets.

- Lesbian couples should be aware of and sympathetic towards their partner if she suffers from pre-menstrual syndrome. Often when two women live together for extended periods of time, their menstrual cycles coincide and this can be difficult to deal with if both partners suffer from PMS.
- Try not to bring your work or any problems associated with it home with you.

These guidelines are really only commonsense but they can be easily forgotten if things are not working out. Remember it is better and easier to sort these things out at the beginning of a relationship rather than wait for a crisis to happen.

Money

It is imperative that same-sex couples sort out who owns what from the start. Cars, flats, houses, furnishing – in fact all major items bought together must be discussed and the arrangements put down on paper. This will prove invaluable not only in the event of a break-up but also in the event of the death of your partner. If your partner dies without making a will his/her belongings automatically go to the next of kin. You will get nothing unless specifically stated in the last will and testament of your partner. It may seem morbid to discuss such matters or you may even be afraid of tempting fate but it is vital that they are sorted out at an early stage of the relationship so as to avoid possible confusion and heartbreak later on.

Dealing with a break-up

It is a sad fact of life that relationships come to an end. Some run their natural course and finish by mutual agreement whereas others end when one partner falls out of love, or into love with someone else. It is important that you deal with your feelings when this happens as you have to grieve for the loss of your relationship. Here are some other commonsense guidelines to help you.

- A quick clean break is easier for you in the long term although it may be more painful in the short term.
- Sort out all your financial dealings as soon as possible. Dragging financial matters out for months will only lead to even more bad feeling.
- Try not to blame your partner. It takes two people to make a successful relationship.
- Don't be pessimistic! Maybe it was meant to be that your relationship broke up. You never know – you could be destined to meet someone even more suited to you.
- Try not to have contact with each other for a while as any contact may open up your wounds.
- Don't turn to drink or drugs as a way of forgetting as all your problems will still be there when you sober up.
- Most importantly, even it is regarded as a cliché, re-member the phrase: 'time really does heal.'

Bear in mind that these are only general guidelines which may not work for you.

13 Bisexuality

You may be reading this book simply because you think you might be lesbian or gay as a result of being attracted to a member of your own sex. Lots of people are attracted to members of their own sex and aren't gay. Sometimes this is a once-off thing, like a crush on a schoolpal or a colleague at work but sometimes they remain attracted to their own sex, as well as to the opposite sex, throughout their lives. People who are attracted to members of both sexes are known as bisexuals.

Some people think that bisexuals are lucky. They can have the best of both the gay and the straight worlds without any of the hassle. But this is not so. A lot of lesbians and gays see bisexual people as 'fence sitters'; that is, they think that they are really gay but are afraid to 'come out' properly. Straight people tend to think of bisexuals in much the same way, or as ditherers who can't make up their minds as to what they want. The bisexual is stuck between both communities without one to call his or her own. When they are in opposite sex relationships, bisexuals are presumed to be heterosexual and when they are in a same sex relationship they are presumed to be gay. Society tends to reject the idea of bisexuality as a legitimate sexual orientation even more than it rejects homosexuality.

If you are bisexual it is as important for you that you

develop a sense of pride about yourself as it is for a lesbian or a gay man. Your sexual desires are just as real, just as important, as heterosexual or homosexual desires.

There are varying degrees of bisexuality. Some bisexuals will *prefer* their own sex while still enjoying opposite-sex activity, some will prefer the opposite sex while still enjoying same-sex activity and others will enjoy both equally. Regardless of which gender you prefer you should not feel forced to choose either a heterosexual or homosexual lifestyle. By doing so you are not only denying your true orientation, that of bisexuality, but denying yourself possible opportunities and experiences. Your life is your own so don't give into any pressure to conform.

Jackie's Story

In my teenage years I thought I was lesbian. All my sexual activity was with other women and I found it very satisfactory. I never once found myself attracted to a man; in fact the thought of sex with a man repelled me. All those disgusting blue veins, you know! Anyway, when I was twenty-three I met Doug and we became friends. He knew I was lesbian as I was going with his sister at the time but that didn't stop him chasing me. The more he persisted, the more he intrigued me and I eventually agreed to meet him for a date. One date led to another and six months later we 'came out' and told my lover, his sister. Initially she went wild, threatening not to speak to either of us again, but as the months passed and she saw how serious we were about each other she relented. She was even bridesmaid for me at the wedding.

After the marriage and between children I felt my longing

for women returning. Don't get me wrong, I still loved Doug very much. It's just that there was something missing from my life, a woman. I talked it over with Doug and to my surprise he said that he knew it would happen eventually and that if it would make me happier I could take a female lover. I suppose he didn't want to lose me to a secret affair. Months passed and I did nothing about finding a lover. It was at the christening of my second child that it happened. I got a little drunk and Pauline, Doug's sister, my ex-lover, ended up in my bed with me. All the old feelings rushed back and it was one of the most exciting sexual experiences of my life. Afterwards I felt tremendous guilt. I mean it was my husband's sister, for God's sake! How was he going to react to that if he found out?

The guilt got the better of me after a while and I told him everything. He was delighted, strangely enough. Somehow the fact that it was his sister made him feel more secure, took away some of the risk of my leaving him. Pauline lives with us now, to the outside world as the nanny, to the children as their aunt and to me as my lover. She has her own room which we use to make love in. Doug has never seen us have sex together and has no wish to so it's not as if it's a sexual fantasy thing with him. I guess I'm just lucky.

John's Story

When I was seventeen I signed up with the army. It was what I always wanted to do. I've always been very well-built – I think it's genetic – very muscular and very fit. The army seemed perfect. My girlfriend at the time didn't want me to join because it meant long periods away from her but I went ahead anyway. It was great. The physical exercise I got made my body develop even further and I started to get admiring glances from both men and women when I walked in the street in uniform. The men made me feel nervous, I didn't like anyone thinking I was a fuckin' queer, not even queers themselves.

Shortly after I completed my training they let me out on leave. I went to this nightclub, I hadn't been there for ages and in the meantime it had turned gay one night a week. I didn't know this and in fact I didn't cop on for a while after I entered since I was fairly drunk. I noticed all the men looking at me, but I thought it was just curiosity at my army-style haircut. When the drink took its toll I had to go to the loo. It was empty except for one guy, about twenty-three, muscular and quite good looking, I suppose. As I was using the urinal I caught him looking at me. Strangely, this turned me on, which was obvious to him. Without a word he went into a cubicle and beckoned me to follow him, which I did, the drink having made me lose any inhibitions I might have had. He went down on me. It felt so natural and it was the best oral sex that I'd ever experienced. When he'd finished I started feeling guilty. I lashed out at him and I think I broke his nose. Before I left the cubicle I landed a kick in his stomach. I know it was wrong but I blamed him for making me this way.

Since then I've learned to accept it. I'm not queer but I *am* bisexual. I prefer women but there are some things that women just can't do and I like those things. I sleep with men only occasionally, in fact I sleep only with one man – he's bisexual as well and we figure that we can meet each other's needs. It saves the hassle of having to go looking for someone when the need arises.

It is not easy to come out as bisexual. As we saw earlier, you may face discrimination from both the straight and the gay communities. It is a decision you should not make lightly and even if you do decide, consider carefully who you tell. Some people who have no problem accepting gay people have difficulties with bisexuals, perhaps because bisexuals are able to integrate into a heterosexual society far more easily than homosexuals and therefore may somehow pose a 'threat' to their cosy little lives.

Bisexuals are wrongly 'blamed' by sections of society for being the conduit that brought AIDS from the gay community into the heterosexual community. This has led to bisexuality, which was once fashionable, being considered 'worse' than homosexuality.

Some psychological theorists hold that every human being is basically bisexual and that both homosexuals and hetero-sexuals are subconsciously repressing one side of their sexuality. This hasn't been proven but it does give us something to think about.

14
Lesbian and Gay Parenting

The fact of being lesbian or gay does not make you unable to have children. There is nothing physically different about us that stops us conceiving a child. Some lesbian and gay couples and even individuals want to have children. If they do not have children from previous relationships they may think about co-parenting a child with a friend who is not their partner or may try to have a baby themselves. There are no set rules for these types of family unit. More and more families are breaking away from the heterosexual two parents and 2.4 kids model. Just because people are lesbian or gay, this does not mean that their sperm ducts and ovaries close down in depression about not having any real use!

Gay parenting has becoming increasingly common in other countries and has become a subject of controversy and media attention, for instance in the case of openly lesbian tennis star Martina Navratilova who declared her intention of trying to have a child when she ended her tennis career. There is also debate (for instance in Britain) about whether the resources of the public health services should be used to arrange artificial insemination for gay women as well as heterosexual women in relationships with men.

If you are a lesbian who wants a child without having a relationship with a man, there are several means open to you.

Artificial insemination

There are two options available in this category. A woman can in theory go to a clinic for artificial insemination by donor. The legal or ethical situation regarding single women is in this country is not clear and we were unable to get a specific answer from anyone in the field in relation to these questions. Alternatively a gay woman can ask a male friend, usually gay, to give her a donation of his sperm. She can inseminate herself, or her lover can do so to share the experience. The sperm is inserted into the body by using a turkey baster or similar object. A baster comprises a long tube with a rubber 'bulb' on the end which, when pressed, squirts the sperm deep into the body. For an increased chance of conception women should monitor their menstrual cycle to find out when they are most fertile.

If you do not know anyone who would become a sperm donor you could advertise in *Gay Community News* or ask some friends for a recommendation. Obtaining sperm from other sources is impossible in Ireland as there is no sperm bank system in operation where you can 'drop in and buy some'. Generally speaking, the medical services in Ireland do not see lesbian couples as a high priority for artificial insemination. Infertile heterosexual couples have more resources and in the view of medical practitioners have more right to receive treatment.

If you decide to proceed with insemination by donor it is vital that you follow a few guidelines. Make sure you know the HIV status of the donor. It is advisable to ask your donor to have an up-to-date test. If he refuses to do so you should consider finding another donor. It is also vital that a contract is made up between you to establish what rights both parties have. If he is to have no involvement in the upbringing of the child then that must be stated so there is no comeback at a later date.

If you are a gay man who is considering donating sperm in an agreement of this sort it is advisable to have a contract stating that you are not liable for maintenance payments for any child that may be conceived. If the donor is to have future rights or a role to play in the child's upbringing then this must be written in a contract also, to minimise the risk of confusion later on.

Karen's Story

I had been living with my girlfriend for five years and we really wanted a child. Her brother, who is gay, agreed to father a child with me. That way it would be the closest thing we could get to a child of our own. I remember it so clearly. He didn't elaborate on how it would be done and neither my girlfriend nor I knew how it was done. We thought I'd have to sleep with him and any time we stayed in his house I'd perch myself on the end of his bed for a 'chat' and wait for something to happen. Of course it never did – he's as gay as they come and could never have sex with a woman. One night I came right out with it and asked him to sleep with me. It was then that he told me about the turkey baster thing. At first I scoffed at the idea, thinking it would never work, but we were desperate enough to try anything.

It was he who suggested the HIV test and the contracts. We'd never have thought of anything like that. Once we'd got that stuff out of the way he moved in with us for a few weeks so we could try whenever the mood took us. He would masturbate himself to orgasm in one room and place the sperm in the baster before giving it to his sister, who would come into our room where I would be masturbating to get myself ready to receive it. She would then place the baster into my vagina and inseminate me, after which we would make love. This we did maybe ten times before we had any success and I conceived – a beautiful baby girl born earlier this year. Both our families know the background to her birth and everyone, including her father, considers her to be our daughter.

Deliberately getting pregnant by a stranger

Alternatively, women both gay and straight have in the past been known to sleep with a stranger with the sole aim of getting themselves pregnant. Obviously they would have known nothing about these men. This can lead to difficulties. If you pick up a man with the intention of having sex in order to conceive, then you are going to be practising unsafe sex. You will not know his sexual history, you will not know if he is an injecting drug user and you will not know his medical history. His HIV status will also be a mystery. These are all risks that you must weigh up before you choose this option. Furthermore, as your child grows up he or she is bound to ask questions about their father, you must be prepared to answer these questions in the way that you see fit. The child will be entitled to know the truth and it is up to you to tell it.

Catherine's story

My girlfriend and I had been together for four years and we
wanted more than anything to have a child. We'd explored
the possibility of fostering but decided there was too much
hassle involved. Then we hit upon the idea of one of us just
sleeping with a man to get pregnant. The only problem was
which one of us. We came to an agreement that both of us
would get men and that would double our chances. Night
after night we hit the straight bars around town but there
must have been something about us that screamed 'lesbian
couple' at the men because they kept their distance. In the
end we had to go out separately.

This one night we both went out and funnily enough we
both scored. It was awful for me. I have nothing against men
but they do nothing for me sexually; they're all beer gut and
foul breath. My girlfriend missed her next period and sure
enough she was pregnant. My period came and went; I wasn't.
To think that I had to sleep with that man and I had nothing
to show for it (my souvenir stubble rash had long since
faded). She gave birth to a healthy boy, whom I loved
immediately despite the pangs of jealousy I felt because it
was she who had given birth and not me.

I eventually got over my jealousy. It was something I
managed to hide from my lover, at least I hope I did. Little
Jonathan is seven years old now. When he started asking
questions about his father, we told him that his father died
before he was born. It's better that way, we think. Maybe
when he's older we'll tell him the truth but somehow I doubt
it. Something like that would be very difficult to absorb,
especially after so long.

Lesbian and gay agreements

Of course if you don't wish to sleep with a stranger there are other ways to get pregnant. Parenting agreements between lesbians and gay men are becoming very popular worldwide. In an agreement of this kind, a lesbian couple and a gay male couple who are close friends arrange to have joint custody of any child conceived between them, usually by artificial insemination. Sometimes both sets of parents would live in the same house but more commonly they have separate residences and the child stays with each set of parents for a fixed time.

Although the cost of bringing up a child conceived in this way would be shared between the two couples and so therefore would be less of a problem, there are some disadvantages. Jealousy can rear its ugly head, with one set of parents envious of the time spent with the other set. The two sets of couples might have different ideas as to how they want to bring up the child, leading to confusion in the child and squabbling among the parents.

This is an option you may want to take but before you do you must think very carefully about all the consequences, especially those that may be unique to your situation.

Adoption

At the moment, adoption is not a viable option due to the prevailing legal and social conditions. Even in countries where lesbian and gay partnerships are officially recognised, a ban has been placed on the right to adopt. The general argument against adoption by lesbian and gay men is that there are many heterosexual couples who cannot adopt due to lack of 'supply'. But is it not the welfare of the child that is paramount and not the sexuality of the parents? Again society's attitudes and homophobia are dictating that the nuclear family is the desirable option. As you can see from this chapter, all types of family units are now in existence in Ireland and the adoption question will no longer be a major issue on the equal rights shopping list.

Accidentally

Not every gay or lesbian parent plans to have a child; some have become parents accidentally. Drink or drugs can be a factor in this but it can also happen when, in an attempt to hide their homosexuality, lesbians or gays have a hetero-sexual experience. Some gay women seem to have the impression that because they are gay they are somehow immune to accidental pregnancy and are therefore careless in practising safe sex during any heterosexual encounters they might have. If you are a lesbian or a gay man who sometimes engages in heterosexual intercourse, you must use some form of contraception if you have no wish to become a parent.

Men co-parenting

As women are regarded as more 'natural' parents, a male couple raising a child faces greater discrimination. Onlookers may express concerns about the wellbeing of the child, while those who do not accept homosexuality may accuse couples of being sexual abusers. These myths will be expounded by bigots and those who are poorly informed about gay life-styles in an attempt to maintain 'family values'. It is important to make sure that you and your family have a support structure of friends to help you cope with isolation. Remember that statistics show that at least 95 per cent of known sexual assaults are carried out by heterosexual men.

Derek's Story

Derek had been going out with a girl, Bernadette, for three months when he first told her he was gay. Divulging this information didn't bring the relationship to an end as one might expect; instead the relationship went on for a further three years before they split. Shortly afterwards, at a party, they both had rather a lot to drink and ended up sleeping together one last time before he emigrated to London. It was there that he got the call to say that Bernadette was pregnant and he came home to discuss their situation. All the options were explored and at one stage they even thought of marriage. In the end, though, they decided to remain single with Bernadette having custody of their son and Derek having full access rights.

Derek is now living back in Dublin and commutes to his home town of Galway regularly to spend time with his son who bears his father's surname. To this day the couple remain the best of friends and cooperate fully in the upbringing of their son, despite the geographical distance between them.

Whichever option you choose you must be careful to weigh

up all the pros and cons. Deciding to have a child is not an easy decision to make, regardless of your sexuality, but being a lesbian or gay parent does lead to some extra difficulties that heterosexual parents don't have to face. You may experience discrimination by other parents, school authorities, social workers and anybody else who feels they have a right to cast judgement.

Lesbian couples who want to have children or indeed have children from previous relationships may wish to contact Lesbians Organising Together (LOT) (See Useful Addresses) for more information and details of support groups they run. It is important to bear in mind that, regardless of which avenue you choose in order to have a child, only one woman will have legal rights over the child or children. Guardianship should be considered for the other partner and you should get in touch with a solicitor specialising in family law for further advice.

15 Married and Gay

Many lesbian and gay people marry heterosexually, either because they haven't yet realised their true orientation or because of a desire to hide their homosexuality from their friends and family. For all their faults, these marriages do have the advantage of giving them the opportunity to have children. However, due to the attitude of the Irish courts, a gay or lesbian parent is unlikely to get any sort of custody of these offspring in the event of an acrimonious split. Sometimes, if one is lucky, these marriages can evolve into an 'open' relationship, after the gay partner has outed him/herself. In this kind of relationship, the partnership remains intact with both partners having the freedom to take other lovers on the side.

Tom's Story

I knew I was gay from an early age, but being from the country I never got the chance to do anything about it. When I was twenty-three I finally gave up hope of meeting someone else who felt the same way as me and I started going out with a girl. As the relationship went on we experimented sexually, just the usual fumblings in the hay barn or the car, that sort of thing. Even though I loved her in my own way, the sex bit didn't do anything for me unless I closed my eyes and dreamed of being with a man. It wasn't so bad. We got married in church, big cars, big reception, foreign honeymoon, the whole works. Everyone thought we were the perfect couple.

As the years went on we had three children, all girls, all beautiful. We moved to Dublin when I got a good job up there. One day I was in a bookshop in the city centre when I saw a free newspaper called *Gay Community News*. I couldn't believe it. I grabbed a copy, stuffed it up my jumper and left as fast as I could. The paper gave me the first knowledge I'd ever had about other gays in Ireland and I couldn't waste that information. I began to visit one of the pubs that was listed as a 'gay' pub and had sex of sorts with a couple of men – in their places obviously, not mine. It wasn't long before the wife started to suspect something was going on, I suppose I got careless, leaving phone numbers around and stuff. When she found a box of condoms and some lubricant in my pocket she went wild – she thought I was having an affair with a woman. I broke down in tears and told her the whole story – the bars, the men, how I was gay – everything. The next day when I came home from work my bags were packed and there was a note saying that she'd gone away for a couple of days and that I was to be gone when she got back. I spent the next day arranging a flat and moved out. That was the last time that I set foot in the family home. She refuses to let me in the door and won't let me see the kids. I have thought about going to court to try and get access rights but I'm afraid of it all being brought out into the open and hurting the kids further. I'm hoping that as time goes on she'll calm down a bit and see that I can't help the way I am. I know I hurt her but, believe me, it wasn't intentional.

There is no divorce in Ireland at present so if a marriage breaks down irretrievably legal separation is the only option available. Although this means that to all intents and purposes the marriage is over, it still denies the heterosexual partner the opportunity to remarry if they wish to do so. This must be taken into account if you are considering marrying to hide your orientation.

Jill's story

I married quite late in life. I was thirty-three when I finally succumbed and walked down the aisle. I didn't want to marry him; I felt that I was betraying his love and trust in me but my friends and family were starting to ask awkward questions about my avoidance of the subject. My girlfriend and I discussed it and we decided that I should go ahead and accept his proposal if only to keep everybody off of our trail. As we came from a rural background, people were starting to get suspicious of our friendship and we thought this would stop the rumours. I knew it wasn't fair on my husband but I was panicking at the time and wasn't really thinking straight.

The marriage lasted only two years before we split acrimoniously but that was enough to convince people that I was indeed 'normal'. My relationship with my girlfriend continued and went from strength to strength until finally we decided that we could hide it no longer and together we found the courage to come out and be counted. The initial reaction from the townspeople was one of rejection but gradually things improved when they saw how committed we are to each other. We have a number of friends now within the local community and find them very supportive.

My ex-husband is living with another woman now. They can never marry because of our marriage and that is something I regret. If only I had had the courage to come out earlier a lot of hurt and sorrow all round would have been avoided.

Paul's story

I always knew I was gay, it never bothered me and I was sexually active at a fairly young age. My parents were staunch Catholics, however, so I could never come out to them no matter what happened. I met a girl I got on really well with and I dated her a few times so they wouldn't get suspicious. She fell in love with me, though. God only knows why – I'm nothing special to look at. I liked her, I didn't love her but I thought that we could make it work if we really tried. We married and I continued to have a gay life unknown to her (I still hadn't told her anything about my past). We had one child, a boy, who's nine now.

I got laid off from my job and that meant I was at home all day on my own while she was at work. I placed a classified ad for men who wanted fun during the day and had a ball for a few weeks until she came home early one day and caught me in bed with some bloke. Far from throwing a fit she just walked from the room and out of the house. When she returned we talked about what had happened and after many tears and much soul-searching we came to the agreement that I could have male lovers if she could have lovers also. It's an arrangement that's worked for us, even brought us closer in some ways. The only jealousy comes into it is if one of us fancies the other one's 'affair', although, having said that, we did share one man between us for a while. My wife and I don't have sex together any more but we'd never part. Our son doesn't have an inkling about our somewhat unorthodox life. We both love him too much to expose him to it and we'd never part from each other, if only for his sake.

Marriage between a lesbian and a gay man

Sometimes, for whatever reason, lesbian women and gay men marry each other. Some do so as a way of hiding their orientation from their respective families and continue to keep up the pretence for some time afterwards. Others do so for legal reasons, such as to obtain a visa so that a friend's partner can remain in the country. In these situations it is advisable to work out everything in advance. Details such as living space, expenses, taxation, social welfare benefits and even the duration of the marriage are vital considerations which must be thrashed out before a wedding takes place. Legal problems can arise from these marriages: for instance, who gets what in the event of a split. The Department of Justice carries out very stringent tests on those who wish to marry Irish citizens, something you must take into account if you plan to do this.

16 Disability

Disabled lesbians and gay men have been the most invisible facet of Ireland's lesbian and gay communities. Some disabilities are hidden, while others are very visible. Disabled people have spent years trying to break through the discrimination brought about by separate education, the patronising attitudes of charitable organisations and the institutional system administered by the religious and the state. In the midst of all this, the issue of sexuality has been firmly swept under the proverbial carpet and stood upon to prevent it creeping back out.

While all disabled people face problems in having their sexuality accepted as a fundamental right, disabled lesbians and gay men face even more discrimination from the non-disabled 'brothers and sisters'. The lesbian and gay scene does not lend itself to an easy coming out for those of us with disabilities. Lack of access, loud music, packed venues, managements reluctant to admit us and the fear and ignorance of other scene-goers can make the isolation even greater.

Gerry's story

My disability is very obvious as I have a curvature of the spine. I can't get out very often and when I do, it requires a lot of help from some friends. Making new friends and finding partners is very hard. It took me years to accept being gay. Now that I want to enjoy my life, I find that able-bodied gay men do not want to have to cope with my disability. When I have been in relationships, my partner has been looked upon as the Good Samaritan. Some people think that he has to be my carer. They talk to him and don't talk to me. They never imagine that we can be in love; in fact they often see me as sexless. I think that other gay men see my extra needs and possible sexual difficulties first before they see me, the gay man who just wants to be accepted in a relationship and who has an awful lot to give.

Jan's story

I am a lesbian with hearing difficulties. Many women do not discover that I am deaf until they start talking to me. I don't wear my hearing aids all the time as I can lip- read very well. The deaf community is not very accepting of lesbians and gay men and I lost a few friends when I told them that I was gay. Lesbian social outlets are often very dark and noisy so when I want to talk to someone I can neither hear them or read what they are saying. There are no groups for deaf or disabled lesbians yet and I am embarrassed to go to other hearing and able-bodied groups as I do not know what to expect. Many see only my disability and no matter how butch I look, fail to recognise me as a lesbian. I cannot use the telephone so there is not even a chance to ring the lesbian line. I wish there was a place I could go.

While the stories above may not reflect everyone's experiences, they do show how people can find life very hard. Sometimes others may not even realise that they are treating disabled people differently because of their disability. Often it is hard to accept the double identity of being gay and disabled but disabled lesbians and gay men are entitled to the same respect and support as any able-bodied person in a lesbian or gay group. Lesbian and gay groups do not discriminate knowingly against disabled members of the community. Many of them may never have been approached by a disabled person for help. As a minority who have been oppressed for decades they should be able to understand the feelings of disabled gay people. As more disabled lesbians and gay men come out, groups are beginning to realise their needs and the facilities they require to benefit from their groups.

If you need help or support in coming out or any other aspect of life get in touch with the nearest Gay Switchboard or Lesbian Line either by phone or post and do not be afraid to ask for advice and information. If you are experiencing difficulties in any gay venue ask your local gay group to help you. They may be able to support you and encourage venues to become accessible. It is time for able-bodied lesbians and gay men to see and hear from disabled members of the gay community. *They are family too!*

17

Some Alternatives to Coming Out

In the past it was almost impossible to come out as lesbian or gay in Ireland; it simply was not done. Lesbian women and gay men had a number of alternatives available at the time, some of which are still prevalent today. Marriage (which we have spoken about in the chapter Married and Gay) was commonplace, and another popular alternative was emigration.

Emigration

Over the years this country has lost many thousands of its talented children as they left its shores to build lives for themselves in countries more tolerant than our own. Emigration is still used as an escape route by some lesbians and gays who see it as their only hope of having a same-sex relationship. Out of sight, out of mind, as the old saying goes. Many who would never have thought it possible to live with their partners in the same country as their parents have no problem setting up home in foreign lands. Once settled abroad these emigrants often found that they were not a welcome part of the Irish community in those countries and so, safe in the knowledge that their families were perhaps thousands of miles away, they set about making their own communities in their new homes. Considerable emigration figures have led to large Irish lesbian and gay communities around the world, the largest of which is probably in New York.

New York

There is a thriving, active Irish lesbian and gay community in New York city. Every year in the run-up to St Patrick's Day, ILGO, the Irish Lesbian and Gay Organisation, puts in an application to partake in the parade through the city. The parade in New York is organised by the Ancient Order of Hibernians, a Catholic group that persistently refuses to allow ILGO entry. Each year ILGO hold a counter-march down a side street as a form of protest against their exclusion and each year the police move with unnecessary force and arrest the peaceful protesters.

Contrast the situation here at home in Ireland. In 1992, following protests by outraged lesbians and gays against the AOH outside the tourism offices in Dublin, the organisers of the St Patrick's Day parade issued an invitation to the lesbian and gay community to take part in the Dublin parade. However, this invitation came too close to the event itself to allow for adequate preparation. In Cork, though, the local lesbian and gay community put together a float for the parade that won the best new entry award.

In 1993 the National Lesbian and Gay Federation took part in the Dublin parade for the first time, accompanied by two television crews from the big American networks, an assortment of photographers from around the world and more than a few uniformed gardaí. Except for a couple of incidents of egg-throwing (organised by declared members of a right-wing youth organisation who were pictured in the act) the parade passed without incident. The NLGF float won a special recognition award. Cork and Galway also had official lesbian and gay entrants in their parades that year. Meanwhile in New York the organisers were still denying their Irish lesbian and gays citizens the opportunity to represent their community on the parade there.

Once again, in 1994, there were entrants in the Cork, Galway and Dublin parades and once again the day passed without major incident. This time however, there was no major media coverage either at home or abroad. It had simply become a matter of fact that lesbians and gays were allowed to enter St Patrick's Day parades in Ireland and march under banners showing the groups that they represented. Nobody batted an eyelid. New York once again witnessed violent scenes as lesbian and gay protesters were arrested. An eyewitness described the scene as 'bloody and horrible. The police just waded in arresting people. Their batons didn't care whether you were male or female. Everyone got treated equally; everyone got a belt of the dreaded nightstick.' Who says the grass is always greener?

Boston

First-generation Irish lesbians and gays along with lesbians and gays of Irish descent organised together and applied to participate in the city's St Patrick's Day parade. The organisers of the parade, The Southern Coalition of Allied Veterans, refused their application. A long court battle ensued, with the gays winning the right to participate. Unfortunately the parade organisers preferred to cancel the parade altogether thus ending a ninety-two-year-old tradition rather than let the Irish lesbians and gays march in it.

San Francisco

San Francisco has a huge lesbian and gay population, made up of people from all over the world. Indeed, in some areas, lesbians and gay men far outnumber the heterosexual population. It will come as no surprise, then, to hear that Irish lesbians and gays were represented in the San Francisco parade with no problems or repercussions whatsoever.

There are Irish lesbians and gays in almost every country on the planet, many of them living the lives that they felt they couldn't have lived here if they had stayed. However, in recent times, and especially since decriminalisation, more and more of them are finding their way back home to the new, more tolerant Ireland.

Visibility

Large numbers of lesbians and gays emigrating has led to a lack of visibility here at home. The community in Ireland should by rights be a lot bigger than it is at present but over the years it has suffered terrible depletion due to emigration. Lack of visibility has a number of side-effects, not least that many people in Ireland do not know that there is an active lesbian and gay community in all of the country's big cities. Young people growing up gay do not know that they are not the only ones. Older people who are still closeted do not know where to go to meet people like themselves.

Since decriminalisation, visibility has increased considerably, with the media suddenly taking an interest in lesbians and gays. Television programmes have been made about lives of some, interviews have been done and radio time has been devoted to us. A result of this has been an increased number of lesbians and gay men coming out and making contact for the first time. Another consequence has been the number of emigrants returning to Ireland, no longer afraid to stand up and be counted.

Paula's Story

I emigrated to London when I was twenty. I had grown up in a small country town and never knew of the existence of any sort of a gay community in Ireland. School was difficult for me. People seemed to know that there was something different about me. They couldn't put their finger on it but they treated me differently just the same. I got a Saturday job in a small record shop and for two years saved the money to emigrate. My parents just thought I was leaving because there was no work in our town.

When I got to London I found the Lesbian Line number in the phone book and after a few weeks plucked up the courage to give them a ring. They put me in touch with a lesbian discussion group in my area but I didn't like it. The idea of being in a room full of women intimidated me. I found out about a lesbian and gay youth group and went to that instead. I was one of only a handful of women there – the men far outnumbered us – but the atmosphere was so much more relaxed. These were people who just wanted to live their lives and have fun. They didn't sit around moaning about how hard their lives were because they were gay. It was like having a new family. When we went out we all looked out for each other. If anyone looked like they needed help we were over to them in a flash. It was great; for the first time in my life I felt a sense of belonging. Nevertheless, I missed Ireland and at the back of my mind I wished I was nearer to home.

When I was itting in a café one day having a coffee, I spotted a young man from my home town. I was mortified as this was a lesbian and gay café, and I tried to leave without his seeing me. Just as I reached the door he saw me and came over. 'I didn't know you were gay,' he said. I nearly died. He was gay as well! If only I'd known sooner – he lived only a couple of minutes from my parents' house. I could have had someone to talk to when we were both growing up. He showed me a copy of *Gay Community News*, which really blew my mind. I mean, a lesbian and gay newspaper in Ireland! He was due to stay in London for two more weeks before returning to his base in Dublin so we spent a lot of time together. When he was leaving we discussed my going to live with him in Dublin and that's exactly what happened. I've been back in Ireland three years now and I don't think I could ever leave again. I have an Irish girlfriend and things are getting better by the day.

Suicide

Studies done in the United States put the figure for young lesbians and gay men committing suicide at 30 per cent of all suicides in America. (No similar study has been done in Ireland.) This is a very high figure considering that the generally accepted percentage of homosexuals in any population is 10 per cent. There are many causes for this: the strain of leading a secret life; the fear of someone finding out; bullying and depression. There is reason to believe that in the past the numbers of lesbians and gay men who committed suicide was even higher than it is now. Many saw it as their only way out, loneliness and isolation making them feel that they would be better off dead.

Suicide is not the solution. Thousands of lesbians and gays have been through the experiences you are going through and they have come out the other end all right and so will you. If you feel that you can't go on, find help. Ring a Lesbian or Gay Switchboard and talk to the volunteer who answers. Alternatively ring the Samaritans. Don't suffer in silence.

18 The Media

Representations of lesbians and gay men in the media have traditionally been few and far between. The national broadcasting organisation hasbeen covering cover gay issues only in the past ten years, but even in that period the efforts have been low-key. It is, of course, vital that people coming out get to see images of lesbians and gay men presented in a positive light so as to provide role models and also to convey the message that they are not alone.

In the past all stories relating to lesbians and gay men were aimed at a heterosexual audience. Lesbians and gays were treated as exhibits to satisfy the curiosity of the masses. Coverage was usually confined to what might be conceived as the negative aspects of the gay community such as 'cruising' and 'cottaging' (having sexual encounters in public toilets). Anything that was considered positive was either ignored or distorted into a threat. Representations of lesbians and gay men in the British tabloid press had a strong influence until, more recently, the tabloids began to publish Irish editions which were not as homophobic in order to cater for changing attitudes in Irish society.

In the past two years, lesbians and gay men have been to the fore in current affairs coverage in the Irish media. Profiles, reports and interviews are generally written in a non-sensationalist way with relatively little evidence of homophobia. Many would even argue that we have become so mainstream that we are now in danger of being ignored. Here are some examples of events in recent lesbian and gay history and the media coverage of them.

Visit to the President at Áras an Uachtaráin

In December 1992, the President of Ireland, Mrs Mary Robinson, invited thirty-four representatives of the lesbian and gay community to her official residence, Áras an Uachtaráin. Within the lesbian and gay community this was perceived to be a major turning-point in the battle for equality. Yet the event was largely ignored by the media. Was it because it was seen as positive and there was no way possible that the media could show positive coverage of an event that involved people who were still legally considered to be criminals? Was it because they thought that the heterosexual audiences might not be interested in this event? Was it because they thought that their lesbian and gay audience was not important enough to be catered for?

Whatever the reason, the media lost a golden opportunity to show gays and lesbians in a positive light.

St Patrick's Day parade

Without a doubt this was the most widely covered gay issue in history before the decriminalisation of homosexuality. All the media devoted large amounts of space to this day, mainly because of the situation in New York and Boston, where Irish gays were banned from taking part in the festivities. Groups from Ireland were invited to take part in the St Patrick's Day Parade in Cork, Limerick and Galway. The Dublin parade and their participation caught the imagination of many journalists. On the run-up to the day the media from all over the world descended on Dublin in an effort to get a story. Yet in the midst of all the hundreds of articles, bulletins, and programmes on this event, not one was aimed at a gay audience. All coverage concentrated on satisfying the curiosity of heterosexual people about gay people. All coverage referred to the gay participants as 'they' or 'them', automatically excluding any lesbian or gay who might have been watching the news or reading the article.

Decriminalisation of homosexuality

Because this issue was ignored by successive governments it was therefore generally ignored by the media. Only when a right-wing activist or member of the hierarchy raised the issue would there be any sort of coverage. In the months leading to the reform of legislation there was coverage of the issues surrounding homosexuality. There again the media created a dog-fight situation, pitching homophobes against homosexuals, and in many cases the programmes degenerated into a squabble.

These are just three examples of how the Irish media used to deal with lesbian and gay issues. In the past year or so, however, things have changed for the better.

RTE

Lesbians and gay men have appeared on the *Late Late Show* and other mainstream programmes as well as making 'Access' community television programmes.

Earlier this year, *Get A Life*, a show aimed at young people and broadcast at teatime, devoted a large segment of one programme to the subject of young lesbians and gays. The show featured a profile of Suzy Byrne (in her capacity as co-chair of the Gay and Lesbian Equality Network, GLEN) and the studio guests were Joan Rippingale (the mother of a gay man), Emma Donoghue (author and TV presenter) and Junior Larkin (in the capacity of leader of the Youth Group Dublin). Although coverage was limited to fifteen minutes, the show was predominantly aimed at any young lesbians or gays who might have been watching and was handled accordingly by the presenter. Phone numbers for both the Gay Switchboard and the Lesbian Line were broadcast at the end of the show. As a result of this programme a number of young lesbians and gays got in touch with the switchboards and made their first contact with other gay people through youth groups, for example.

In other areas also RTE has made progress. On current affairs shows, for example, RTE gets in touch with the gay organisations if there is a topic to be covered that is of interest to gay people. Indeed, when the *Late Late Show* devoted one of its programmes to the topic of young people in Ireland, some young lesbians and gay men were invited to represent their community.

Independent radio

This relatively new sector has shown a lot of interest in lesbian and gay issues. There are currently over twenty independent radio stations in Ireland; these are spread throughout the country and have large audiences. Activists are invited to participate in phone-ins, providing debate and information for listeners. This sector is vital to lesbian and gay men living in rural areas.

Lesbians and gays provide for themselves

Because of the lack of coverage of lesbian and gay issues for lesbians and gay men, community groups have been involved since the late seventies in providing channels of communication for themselves. Whether in the form of newsletters, nationally distributed magazines with a cover price or a free newspaper in the mould of *Gay Community News*, these have become vital links to the community for thousands of lesbians and gay men. *Outwaves*, a programme broadcast on Horizon Radio, was a very successful series that won wide praise for its coverage of lesbian and gay issues. Pressure groups tried to have the show dropped from the station's schedules but they were not successful. The show stopped going out because the volunteers involved had other commitments.

Gay Community News

Since its first appearance in 1989, *GCN* has been published monthly by the National Lesbian and Gay Federation with a current print-run of 6,000 copies and an estimated readership of 13,000. The paper is widely distributed throughout Ireland and has a large international mailing list. Staffed by volunteers and employees of a FÁS Community Enterprise scheme, the paper has been through many crises in relation to funding. The staff put hours into production to get *GCN* on the street.

The paper is divided into sections on news, health and lifestyles, features and broad coverage of arts and culture. With a large classifieds section and comprehensive listings, it provides an invaluable source of information. The paper depends a great deal on voluntary effort but it continues to improve, and while it is not the definitive answer to the need for a lesbian and gay print journal, there have been no other attempts to replace or improve on this particular newspaper. You will find the paper in most lesbian and gay venues and can also get it by subscription. Write to *Gay Community News* at The Hirschfeld Centre, 10 Fownes Street, Dublin 2.

Publishing

Since the decriminalisation of homosexuality there has been an increased interest in publishing books in Ireland for lesbians and gay men. Publishing houses like Basement Press are developing lesbian and gay lists. Basement Press is an imprint of the well known feminist house, Attic Press. Basement's titles include *One in Every Family*, a book that attempts to dispel the myths about lesbians and gay men, for parents, friends and families of lesbians and gay men.

Also *Quare Fellas*, an anthology of Irish gay writing and *Sugar and Spice*, a collection of Irish women's writing. As well as *Coming Out*, Martello has on its list *Alternative Loves*, an anthology of classic Irish gay and lesbian stories edited by David Marcus.

In 1994, Cork University Press published a pamphlet detailing the history of lesbian and gay politics in Ireland. *Diverse Communities* by Kieran Rose explores how the lesbian and gay community through the last twenty years has fought the battle for equality. The details of the decriminalisation of homosexuality and how it was achieved are also included. Other titles include *Lesbian and Gay Visions of the 21st Century*, edited by Ide O'Carroll and Eoin Collins. This is from Cassells, a British company with a very good reputation in gay publishing.

19 Private Life – Public Eye

Traditionally, people in the public eye in Ireland have preferred to keep their private lives private. Lesbians and gays especially – and not surprisingly – have kept their private lives under wraps, with the result that there is a lack of role models for young lesbian and gay people. In Ireland, even today, there is a disappointing lack of openly gay public figures, although the aituation is gradually improving.

Emma Donoghue

Perhaps Ireland's highest profile lesbian (out lesbian that is) Emma has come to public attention only in the last couple of years. Still in her early twenties, Emma has had two books published, and her lesbian play, *I know my Own Heart*, was staged in 1993 to mostly positive reviews. After publishing her first novel, *Stir Fry*, Emma was offered a job as co-presenter of *Books 94*, RTE television's book show, thereby further increasing her profile.

Emma has been openly gay right from the start of her literary career and while much has been made of her lesbianism in the media it has not damaged her career. Her output so far has been gay-themed yet not confined to a gay readership, as has happened to the work of other writers in the past. Emma is not one to dodge questions on her sexuality and hardly an interview goes by without the topic being raised and openly discussed.

Zrazy

Ireland's only openly lesbian musical group Zrazy has achieved much critical acclaim recently. Once again they have been openly gay from the start of their success and are perfectly willing to discuss questions around their sexuality. In 1993 their single *I'm in Love With Mother Nature* received widespread airplay and spread their fan base beyond the lesbian and gay community.

Martin McCann

Lead singer in the Internationally acclaimed Dublin Indie Group *Sack*, Martin McCann is gay and proud of it. Much media space has been given to the band, with interviews sometimes concentrating more on Martin's sexuality than on the group's music. The other (heterosexual) members of the band do not mind this and the band's lyrics, although not written by McCann, sometimes have gay themes.

David Norris

David Norris was for many years known as the 'only gay man in Ireland'. A lecturer in English in Trinity College, he championed the cause of the gay community in Ireland, working hand-in-hand with many people who were unable to be such public activists to advance the rights of gay men.

He was also instrumental in the establishment of the Lesbian and Gay Community Centre (The Hirschfeld Centre), which opened in 1979.

In 1980 David began a long battle in the Irish courts to get the government to change legislation which criminalised gay male sexual activity. Although he lost the case both in the High Court and the Supreme Courts, he finally succeeded in breaking through in the European Court of Human Rights in 1988. David Norris had won the respect of human rights activists throughout the world. Elected to the Seanad in 1989, he has become a notable public representative speaking out on issues concerning human rights abuses in many countries, notably East Timor. One of the most important days of his life was the day on which he himself spoke in the Oireachtas on the bill to decriminalise homosexuality. Nowadays he is not alone in the position of the 'out' gay man and devotes his energies as a public man to many other issues as well.

Lesbian and gay activists

These are people who, although they may not be celebrities, are willing to speak out for equal rights. Kieran Rose and Chris Robson amongst others became fairly well known faces on our TV screens and newspaper pages during the campaign for law reform. Activists play the role of spokespeople for the lesbian and gay community. The visibility that they provide is vital to many young people, straight or gay, who need to see this visibility to challenge homophobia.

In the closet?

Without doubt there is a substantial number of public figures who are lesbian or gay but who keep their sexuality hidden. Many politicians, TV personalities, musicians, writers are 'open secrets' in the gay community; that is, they are 'openly' gay within the confines of the lesbian and gay community but to the general public their sexual orientation is not confirmed. Why is this? Fear seems to be a major cause of this secrecy. The politicians fear losing electoral support; TV personalities may fear losing their audience or indeed their contracts. They don't know what would happen if they did come out, so they are unwilling to take the risk. Instead, they remain under a veil of secrecy, always in fear of being 'outed'. Contrast this with those who have chosen to be out from the beginning. No fear of being outed, no secrecy, no worries.

If there is nothing hidden there is nothing to keep hidden. It seems that if you yourself treat your being lesbian or gay as nothing special, as just another part of you, then other people will see it that way too. There can be no scandal if there is no secret.

20 Community Groups

There are many groups up and running around Ireland with the sole aim of helping lesbian and gay people to live full and satisfying lives. Ranging from social groups for those under the age of twenty-five right through to campaigning groups wishing to achieve full equality in law, there will be an organisation to help you no matter what your problem is. Many colleges and universities have lesbian and gay societies for their students. Here we give you a brief description of what these various groups do. To contact them please refer to the Useful Addresses section on page 138.

The National Lesbian and Gay Federation (NLGF)

Based in the Hirschfeld Centre in Dublin, the NLGF is the publisher of *Gay Community News*, Ireland's only lesbian and gay newspaper. The NLGF also maintains a comprehensive media archive which records the media treatment of lesbians and gays over the past twenty years. On request, the NLGF provides spokespeople to give media interviews, or workshops in schools, colleges and community groups.

The Gay and Lesbian Equality Network (GLEN)

GLEN is a campaigning group set up with the sole intention of achieving law reform. The group has had great success in the past in relation to decriminalisation and employment legislation, and is now concentrating its efforts on the achievement of equal status for lesbians and gay men. The group has the mandate of the entire community and hosts an open day every year to which interested parties can come and tell GLEN what they think their objectives should be. A sister network, the Lesbian Equality Network, was formed in 1993 to campaign on lesbian equality issues including custody and partnership.

Gaeilgeoirí Aeracha Aontaithe (GAA)

The GAA is the group for lesbians and gays who like to speak Irish in a social setting. They have regular meetings where Irish is spoken and welcome people of all levels of fluency.

Lesbians Organising Together (LOT)

LOT is an umbrella organisation for a number of lesbian groups in Dublin. Comprising a finance group, publishing group, a mothers' group, and a social and entertainments group amongst others, LOT aims to improve the lives of lesbian women in Ireland. The organisation is rapidly developing in tandem with increased lesbian visibility. LOT is also responsible for the Wild and Wonderful Women's Weekend which takes place each year in September.

Parents' Enquiry

Parents' Enquiry is a support group run by parents of lesbians and gay men for the parents of lesbians and gay men. The group provides a listening ear whenever someone needs it. It also provides spokespeople for media work. Working closely with Youth Group Dublin, Parents' Enquiry has indirectly helped lots of young people to come out in the knowledge that there is someone for their parents to talk to.

Gay Switchboards and Lesbian Lines

These groups have been running for over fifteen years in one form or another. They are staffed by trained volunteers who provide a listening ear and a first step for many into the lesbian and gay community. In rural areas they provide information for locals and visitors alike on current happenings on the gay scene. They also help those in trouble by giving them the names of professionals who are gay or gay-friendly. Currently there are Lesbian Lines and Gay Switchboards in Belfast, Derry, Dublin, Cork, Galway and Limerick. There is also a service covering the south-east of Ireland.

Icebreakers and First Out

These groups are generally run by those who operate switchboards and lesbian lines. They are meetings for gays and lesbians who are coming out and exploring their sexuality. Facilitators lead discussions and provide information on the lesbian or gay scene and on safer sex. Those who attend have often been referred by a Switchboard or Lesbian Line and can attend for a number of weeks until they feel comfortable about making their own way into the world.

Regional support groups

These groups have been established in several towns and cities. They provide an essential space for meeting other lesbians and gay men for those who are not able or who do not want to come to larger cities. Several of these groups have been started in cooperation with the National Lesbian and Gay Federation. The groups are independent and decide for themselves on structures and activities. Groups are currently on the go in Drogheda, Kerry, Sligo, Waterford, Wexford.

Cork, Limerick and Galway all have a number of groups and organisations for lesbians and gay men. Events such as the Cork Women's Weekend and the Lesbian and Gay Film Festival are highlights of the gay calendar.

Youth groups

These groups are run for and by young lesbians and gay men. They provide a safe space for those under twenty-five to meet and share experiences about coming out. Information on coming out, safer sex and lesbian and gay lifestyles is also given in the form of workshops. Lesbian and gay films and programmes on gay issues which have been shown on television are also shown, as many members would not have the opportunity to see these at home. Generally the groups provide a social setting for young lesbians and gay men where none other is available. Participating in such a group is often the first step for many young people towards accepting themselves and many lasting friendships come about because of the relaxed atmosphere of these groups.

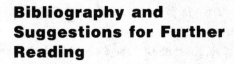

Bibliography and Suggestions for Further Reading

Boston's Women's Health Collective. *The New Our Bodies, Ourselves.* London: Penguin, 1989.

Harbeck, Kay. *Coming Out of the Classroom Closet.* New York: Harrington Park Press, 1991.

Gay Community News. Published monthly by the National Lesbian and Gay Federation, Dublin.

Gocros, Scharrj. *When Husbands Come Out of the Closet.* New York: Harrington Park Press, 1992.

Irish Council For Civil Liberties. *Equality Now for Lesbians and Gay Men.* Dublin: ICCL, 1990.

Trenchard, Lorraine. *Being Lesbian.* London: Gay Men's Press, 1989.

Union of Students in Ireland. *Welfare Guide.* Dublin: USI, 1993.

Further reading

Most of the following can be found at a lesbian and gay section of any of the bookshops listed in the Useful Addresses section. If you cannot find them you should be able to order them. We include a short list of fiction but please remember that there is much more available in the bookshops. We have also have put together a list of books on other areas. This list is by no means comprehensive or definitive, just a sample of what is on offer.

Irish interest

Dublin Lesbian and Gay Collective. *Out for Ourselves: the lives of Irish lesbians and gay men.* Dublin: Women's Community Press, 1986.
Rose, Kieran. *Diverse Communities, The evolution of lesbian and gay politics.* Cork: Cork University Press, 1994.
Fiction
Cullen, Linda. *The Kiss.* Dublin: Attic Press, 1985.
Donoghue, Emma. *Stirfry.* London: Hamish Hamiliton, 1994.
Lennon, Tom. *When Love Comes to Town.* Dublin: O'Brien Press, 1993.
Morrison, Danny. *On the Back of the Swallow.* Cork and Dublin: Mercier Press, 1994.
Marcus, David, ed. *Alternative Loves: Irish Lesbian and Gay Stories.* Dublin: Martello Books, 1994.

Irish magazines that cover lesbian and gay issues on a regular basis.

Hot Press
In Dublin
The Big Issue

British gay publications on sale in Ireland

Attitude
Diva (lesbian)
Gay Times

Video

HMV, Tower Records and virgin Megastore have lesbian and gay video sections. Here you will find feature-length movies, also videos on safer sex and documentaries on aspects of lesbian and gay life.

Films

The following is a short list of films with lesbian or gay themes that you might be able to hire from your local rental shop or watch on television:

Maurice

Sebastian

Desert Hearts

Torch Song Trilogy

Thelma and Louise

Philadelphia

My Own Private Idaho

Orlando

Useful Addresses

National organisations

NLGF (National Lesbian and Gay Federation)
(01) 671 0939 (12-5.30pm)
The Hirschfeld Centre, 10 Fownes St, Dublin 2.
Publishes *Gay Community News*, provides information, maintains a comprehensive media archive and an outreach programme.
Body Positive
(01) 671 2363
4, Dame House, 24-26 Dame St, Dublin 2.
Self-help and support group for people affected by HIV or AIDS.
Employment Equality Agency
(01) 660 5966
36 Upper Mount St, Dublin 2
Deals with cases of job discrimination.
Gaeilgeoirí Aerach Aontaithe (Irish-speaking gay group)
F/C Roy Ó Gealbháin, Ionad Hirschfeld, 10 Sráid Fobhnai, BAC 2
GLEN (Gay and Lesbian Equality Network)
(01) 671 0939 (12.00-5.30pm)
c/o Hirschfeld Centre, 10 Fownes St, Dublin 2.
Group lobbying for law reform.
Irish Congress of Trade Unions
(01) 668 0641
19 Raglan Road, Dublin 4.
Lesbian and gay rights in the workplace.
Irish Names Quilt
(01) 873 3799

53 Parnell Square, Dublin 1.

Quilt in memory of those who have died of AIDS-related illness.

Rights Commissioner Service

(01 660 8444

Labour Relations Commission, Tom Johnson House, Haddington Road, Dublin 4

Agency that runs tribunals to deal with unfair dismissals cases.

LOT (Lesbians Organising Together)

(01) 872 7770

Meets second Thursday of the month at 7pm c/o 5 Capel Street. Umbrella organisation for numerous lesbian groups specialising in different areas.

Parents' Enquiry

Support and information for and by parents of lesbians and gays. Contact Gay Switchboard Dublin.

Union of Students in Ireland

Lesbian, gay. bisexual rights officer and committee. Telephone (01) 6710088 for further details.

Dublin

Organisations

Dublin City University, Lesbian and Gay Society.

Meets Thursdays 6pm. Contact Students Union Office.

First Out

Confidential support group for women exploring their sexuality, discussion facilitated by trained volunteers who are lesbian. First Wednesday and third Saturday each month 7.30 pm. Contact Lesbian Line or Gay Switchboard Dublin for details.

Hirschfeld Outdoors Group

Hiking group. Meets 11am last Sunday of the month at 10 Fownes St, Dublin 2.

Icebreakers

Informal meeting for gays and lesbians coming out. Meets 7.30pm first Saturday every month in city centre hotel. Contact Gay Switchboard Dublin.

Julian Fellowship
> (01) 492 2843
> PO Box 1871, Churchtown, Dublin 14. Thursday 7.30–9pm only.
> First and last Thursday of the month only.
> Support and self-development for Christian lesbian women.

Kevin Street College Lesbian and Gay Society
> Meets every second Wednesday. Contact Students Union Office.

Muted Cupid Theatre Group
> Meets Tuesdays 7.30pm upstairs Rumpoles Bar, Parliament St.
> Write c/o Hirschfeld Centre, 10 Fownes Street, Dublin 2.

Reach
> (01) 492 2843
> PO Box 1790, Dublin 6. Thursday 7.30-9pm only.
> Gay Christian group, meets monthly on Saturday in Dublin.

TCD Lesbian, Gay and Bi Soc.
> Meets Room 626, Thursday. 7.30pm.

The Thursday Club
> Dining club for gay men. Meets second and fourth Thursday of
> each month.

UCD Lesbian and Gay Society
> Contact Students Union for further details.

Youth Group Dublin
> Social group for under 25s, run by young lesbians and gays for
> young lesbians and gays. Meets first and third Sunday. Details
> National Lesbian and Gay Federation or Gay Switchboard Dublin.

Help and Health

Gay Switchboard Dublin (GSD)
> (01) 872 1055
> Carmichael House, North Brunswick St, Dublin 7.
> Sunday–Friday 8–10pm, Saturday 3.30–6.00pm.
> Lesbian Line
> (01) 661 3777
> Thursday 7–9pm.

National Transvestite Line
> (01) 671 0939 Thursday 7–10pm.

Alcoholics Anonymous
> Lesbian and gay group meets Monday 8pm. Contact Lesbian Line
> or Gay Switchboard Dublin for details.

AIDS Helpline Dublin
 (01) 872 4277
 Monday–Friday 7–9pm, Saturday 3–5pm.
Baggot Street Clinic
 (01) 660 2149
 19 Haddington Rd Dublin 4
 Advice, counselling and HIV testing.
Cairde
 (01) 873 0006 daily
 25 Mary's Abbey, Dublin 7
 Voluntary group providing emotional and practical support to
 people who are HIV-positive or have AIDS.
Dublin AIDS Alliance
 (01) 873 3799
 53 Parnell Square, Dublin 1.
Gay Men's Health Project
 (01) 660 2149
 Tuesday and Wednesday, 8–9.30pm. Drop-in, no appointment
 needed.
Holistic Health Project
 (01) 873 3799
 c/o Dublin AIDS Alliance. Holistic massage, shiatsu, relaxation
 sessions for people affected by HIV or AIDS.
St James's Hospital GU Clinic
 (01) 453 5245 (direct line) or (01) 453 7941 ext. 2315/2316
 Hospital 5, Rialto Entrance Monday and Friday 9am–12.30pm.
 Tuesday and Thursday 1:30–4.30pm
 HIV Clinic (01) 453 5245 (direct line) or (01) 453 7941 Ext 2161.
 Monday 1:30–4.30pm. and Wednesday 9am–12pm (HIV+ only).

Bookshops
Books Upstairs
 (01) 679 6687
 36 College Green, Dublin 2.
Irish Family Planning Association
 (01) 872 5366
 36-37 Lower Ormond Quay, Dublin 1.

Waterstones
(01) 679 1415
7 Dawson St, Dublin 2.
The Winding Stair
(01) 873 3292
40 Lower Ormond Quay, Dublin 1.
Bookshop/Café

Accommodation

Frankie's
(01) 478 30 87
8 Camden Place, Dublin 2.
The Horse and Carriage Hotel
(01) 478 3537/478 3504. Fax 478 4010
15 Aungier St, Dublin 2.

Eats

The Cellary
Fownes St, Dublin 2.
Demi-veg restaurant.
Marks Bros
7 South Great George's St, Dublin 2.
Monday–Saturday 10am–5.30pm.
Young, trendy, Mixed gay/straight coffee shop.
The George Bar and Bistro
89 South Great George's St, Dublin 2.
Food served 12–8pm, Monday–Friday.
Lunchtime specials every day.
The Bistro Pizza and Pasta
5 Castlemarket, Dublin 2.
Open till 2am at weekends.
Comfortable mixed restaurant
Sinners Restaurant
12 Parliament St, Dublin 2.
Gay-friendly. Lebanese food.
Well Fed Restaurant
Dublin Resource Centre, 6 Crow St, Dublin 2.
12–8pm Monday–Saturday.
Vegetarian food.

Cibo's Italian Restaurant
17A Lower Baggot St Dublin 2
(01) 676 2050.
7 days. Gay-friendly.

Nightclubs

Shaft
22 Ely Place, Dublin 2
Nightclub and wine bar every night, mixed gay/straight.
The Shelter in The Temple of Sound
Ormond Hotel, Ormond Quay, Dublin 1.
Wednesday 10.30 till late.
The Playground in The Temple of Sound
Ormond Hotel, Ormond Quay, Dublin 1.
Sunday 10.30 till late.
The Block
The George, South Great George's St, Dublin 2.
11pm-2am Friday and Saturday (winter), Wednesday through to
Sunday (summer). Dance Club with full bar.
Boogie an Domhain
PoD
Thursday 11-2.30am. Full bar.
Horny Organ Tribe (HOT)
Rock Garden.
Sunday 11-2.30am. Full bar.
The Salon at The Cellary
Fownes St, Dublin 2.
Saturday 9.30pm-3am. Women only. Food and drink available.
For other women-only venues contact Dublin Lesbian Line.

Pubs

The George
South Great George's St, Dublin 2
The Bailey
2 Duke St, Dublin 2.
Saturday afternoon, mixed, popular with lesbians and gays.

Saunas

The Gym
(01) 679 5128

14-15 Dame Lane, Dublin 2.
Incognito
    (01) 478 3504
    1-2 Bow Lane East (off Aungier St), Dublin 2.

Cork

Organisations

Cork Gay Collective (Icebreakers)
    Meets 8pm monthly last Tuesday.
    Contact Lesbian/Gay Line
Lesbian and Gay Resource Group
    The Other Place, 7-8 Augustine St.
    (021) 317660

Help and Health

Cork Lesbian Line
    (021) 271087
    Thursday 8-10pm
Gay Information Cork
    (021) 271087
    Wednesday 7-9pm and Saturday 3-5pm
Alcoholics Anonymous
    'Live and let live' group; phone Lesbian Line or Gay Information
    Cork.
AIDS Helpline Cork
    (021) 276676
    Monday-Friday 10am-5pm.
STD Clinic, Victoria Hospital
    (021) 966844
    Monday 5.30-7.30pm; Wednesday 10am-12pm.
Cork AIDS Alliance/Cairde
    (021) 275837
    16 Peter's St, Cork.
Reach
    (021) 291371
    Tuesday 7.30-9pm.

Gay Christian Group.
(c/o PO Box 1790 Dublin 6.)

Bookshops

The Other Place Library
Augustine St (by Queen's Old Castle).
Quay Co-Op
(021) 317660
24 Sullivan's Quay.
Waterstone's
(021) 276002
69 Patrick St.

Accommodation

Amazonia B & B
(021) 831115
Coast Road, Fountainstown, Co Cork.
12 miles west of city. Warm welcome for gays and lesbians
Mont Bretia B & B.
(028) 336 63
Adrigole, Skibbereen, Co Cork. Lesbian and gay friendly
(women-run.)

Eats

Quay Co-Op
(021) 317660
24 Sullivan's Quay.
The Other Place (Café)
Augustine St (by Queen's Old Castle).
The Art Hive
McCurtain St.
Art Gallery cum café. Gay-friendly.

Pubs

Loafers
Douglas St.

Nightclubs

The Other Place.
Augustine St.
Saturday night disco; also women's disco first Friday each month.

Belfast

Organisations

NIGRA (Northern Ireland Gay Rights Association)
(0232) 664111/325851.
PO Box 44, Belfast BT1 1SH.
  Meets Thursday 8pm. Also operates lending library.
The Drop-In Centre
  Cathedral Buildings, Lower Donegall Street (next to Spice of Life cafe)
  Sat 1.30-5pm, ring bell marked CF.
Gay Star
  PO Box 44, Belfast BT1 1SH.
  Independent quarterly newsletter from Belfast. £5 annual subscription.
Lesbian and Gay and Bi Youth Group
  (0232) 665257 or 234122.
  Group for under 25s. Meets every Sunday 7.30pm.
Northern Ireland Gay Christian Fellowship
  PO Box 44, Belfast BT1 1SH.
  Meets second and fourth Sunday at 3pm in Cathedral Buildings, 64 Donegall Street.
Belfast Butterfly Club
  PO Box 210 Belfast BT1 1BG.
  Helpline (08494) 69715, Wed 8-10pm.
  Group for transvestites and transexuals.
  Meets 1st and 3rd Tues 8-11.30pm.
  Produces *ITV Magazine*.
Lesbian and Gay and Bisexual Society
  Belfast Institute of Further Education. Contact Damien, Brunswick St College Wednesday 4.30-8.30pm at (0232) 249705.

Help and Health

Cara-Friend Phoneline
(0232) 322023. Monday–Wednesday 7.30–10pm.
Lesbian Line Belfast
  (0232) 238668.

Thurs 7.30-10pm.
Northern Ireland AIDS Helpline
(0232) 326117.
Monday, Wednesday, Friday 7.30-10pm; Sat 2-5 pm.
Parents' Enquiry
(0232) 466944.
Monday and Friday 7.30-10pm.
GUM Clinic (STD Clinic) Royal Victoria Hospital
(0232) 320159. Social Worker 240503 ext 2450.
Health Adviser 328222.
Monday-Friday, 9-11am. Monday, Wednesday and Friday, 2-3pm.

Bookshops
Just Books
(0232) 225426
7 Winetavern St.

Pubs
Crow's Nest Bar
Skipper St (off High St)
Mixed Clientele, Monday to Saturday.
Thursday-Saturday late bar and disco.
The Queen's Bar
Monday to Thursday till 11pm, Friday and Saturday till late.
Friendly atmosphere, mixed clientele.

Nightclubs
Limelight
Ormeau Avenue.
Disco Monday 9pm-1.00am.

Galway

Organisations
PLUTO, UCG Lesbian, Gay and Bi Group.
Thursday during term, 8-10pm.
All UCG/RTC students and others welcome.
Details from Gay/Lesbian Lines.

Ensemble Youth Group
    Meets monthly. Ring lines for details.
Help and Health
Drop-in Centre.
    Opening Saturday afternoons. Contact Gay Line for details.
Galway Gay Help Line.
    (091) 66134.
    PO Box 45.
    Tuesday–Thursday 8–10pm.
Galway Lesbian Line
(091) 66134
    PO Box 45.
    Wednesday 8–10pm.
    Contact for info on basketball, videos, discussion groups.
AIDS Help West
    (091) 66266
    Ozanam House
    (Education, Cairde, Body Positive, Family Support Group
        Helpline)
    Monday–Friday 10–12am, Thursday 8–10pm.
Bookshops
Sheela-na-Gig
    (091) 66849
The Galway Bookshop
    Cornstore Mall, Middle St.
Pubs
Waterfront
    Ravens Terrace (off Dominic St)
    Straight Pub. Gay-friendly

Limerick

Help and Health
Gay Switchboard Limerick
    (061) 310101.
    Monday, Tuesday 7.30-9.30pm.

Lesbian Line Limerick
    (061) 310101.
    Thurs 7.30–9.30pm.
Lesbian and Gay Youth Group.
    Social outlet for people in their teens to mid-twenties. Meets
    every 2 weeks. Contact Gay Switchboard for details.
Limerick Forum.
    Social meetings for gays, lesbians and bisexuals. Meets every
    second Wednesday 8.30pm.
    All welcome. Details from Gay Switchboard
Limerick Gay and Lesbian Film Club.
    Contact Switchboard for details.
Women's Meeting
    Thursday nights.
    Contact Limerick Lesbian Line.
Limerick AIDS Alliance
    PO Box 103, Cecil St, Limerick.
Limerick AIDS Helpline
    (061) 316661.
    Monday–Thursday 7.30–9.30pm.

Derry

Organisations
Drop-In-Centre
    Women's Centre, London Street
    Saturday 2.30–4.30pm
Lesbian and Gay Line NW
    (0504) 263120.
    Thursday 7.30–10pm.
    c/o PO Box 44, Belfast BT1 1SH.
Bookshops
Bookworm
    (0504) 261616
    16 Bishop Street.

Drogheda

Outcomers
   Drogheda's social group for gay men and lesbians. Meets second
   and fourth Friday of month 7-9pm in Resource Centre for the
   Unemployed, 7 North Quay.
   Contact GSD for info.

Sligo

Pubs

Silver Swan (Hotel) Bar Hyde Bridge.
   Mixed, many gays at weekend.

Organisation

Gala (Gay and Les Association) Sligo
   Meets every month.
   c/o Hirschfeld Centre, Dublin.

Waterford

Waterford Assembly
   PO Box 24, GPO Waterford.
   Social group meets in Waterford City on Saturday at 8.30pm.
   Details from local Gay Switchboard or Lesbian Line.
Lesbian Line South East
   (051) 79907.
   Monday 7.30-9.30 pm.
Gay Line south-east
   (051) 79907.
   Wednesday 7.30-9.30 pm.
Parents' Information
   Contact local Gay and Lesbian Switchboard above.

Kilkenny

Eats
The Motte Restaurant
(056) 58655.
Inistioge, Co Kilkenny.
Limited B & B, 15 miles from city.

Kerry

Group for lesbians and gay men meets second Tuesday and fourth Friday in Tralee. Telephone (01) 671 0939 or Switchboards for info.

Britain

Cairde
Social and support group for Irish Lesbians living in London.
Contact (071) 837 2782/837 3337 for further details.
Irish Gay Helpline
(081) 983 4111.
Information and befriending service. Monday 7.30-10pm.
Write BM IGH, London WC1N 3XX.
Irish Gay Dynamic Network
(071) 603 3949/837 0713.
Meets on first and third Tuesday at the the Kings Arms (upstairs), Poland St, W1.
London Lesbian and Gay Switchboard
(071) 837 7324.
Open 24 hours a day, 7 days a week.

USA
ILGO (Irish Lesbian and Gay Organisation) New York
(212) 967 7711 ext 3078.

Conclusion

OK, you have come to terms with your sexuality and are wondering what to do next. The simple answer would be to say: get on with your life and enjoy it. But take your time in doing so. Too many people rush into too many things when they first come out. For instance if you are interested in becoming involved in a lesbian and gay community group don't pick the first one you come across. Examine a number of them before picking the one most suited to you. You will be of far more benefit if you concentrate your efforts.

Also try to avoid the 'feast after the famine' syndrome: making up for the time lost to you whilst in the closet. This causes rapid burn-out and can leave you feeling disillusioned and downhearted with both yourself and the community.

Although you may have come out to your friends and family you must also remember that coming out is an on-going process – something you will have to continue to do for the rest of your life as you meet new people, find a new job or move to a new area. Of course it gets easier as you go along; especially if you have already told other people and got positive reactions.

Whatever happens from now on, you've taken the first step by buying this book. The rest is up to you. You may decide that the time isn't right after all for you to come out or you may decide to go for it. We wish you the best of luck.